# Big Type

Contents:

| | |
|---|---:|
| Intro | 2 |
| Scale | 5 |
| Repeat | 55 |
| Crop | 73 |
| Interact | 109 |
| Condensed | 135 |
| Stretch | 169 |
| Lettering | 193 |
| Colophon | 224 |

Counter-Print Books

Big Type

Throughout time, alphabets and their constituent letters have been the communicative devices of society and have been responsible for the creation of the scribe, calligrapher, typographer and modern graphic designer. The purpose of such alphabets is to give a visual structure to experiences, memory and abstract thought. It is a standardised set of basic written symbols that represent the phonemes of certain spoken languages. Correspondingly, a typeface is the design of lettering that can include variations, such as extra bold, bold, regular, light, italic, condensed, extended, etc. Each of these variations of the typeface is a font. Today, in his search for a typeface, the graphic designer may have a general style in mind or they may have an endless quest on their hands, looking for the typeface that speaks with exactly the right tone of voice. In either case the typeface is chosen for its graphic expression and is often subject to the trends and fashions of the time.

The graphic designer's use of typography changed radically throughout the 20th century. The clean lines and asymmetry of the 1920's, associated with the De Stijl and Bauhaus periods, brought with them a proliferation of sans-serif typefaces which have impacted on design until this day. Significant factors in the spread of this style were the enormous strides and levelling influence of transportation and television during the post war years.

In tandem with this, we witnessed an increasing separation between the visual appearance of type as we see it and type as a structure, as the typesetter would have seen it. This was facilitated by changes from printed type to photographic compositions and then to digital reproduction techniques. Such rapid change has led to a graphic landscape unrecognisable to someone living 100 years ago.

In the 1920's, the function of typography was outlined as solving reading and visual problems. Today, type design, influenced by both strides in technology and a dizzying series of artistic 20th Century periods, has gained a freedom in terms of composition, size, emphasis, colour, weight, spacing etc that would have been inconceivable before.

Of course, all of this progress has not meant that type no longer has (at times) to be legible. The modern graphic designer still needs to have respect for the function of reading. As master typographer Emil Ruder put it, 'the printed word that cannot be read becomes a product without purpose'. However, modern typography must grab and hold our attention, ask us to solve visual riddles, give us pleasure and, at the same time, convey a coherent message.

The increased significance of typography as a tool of world-wide communication is in part down to the fact that information which we hear can be easily forgotten while visual experiences, read and understood, can make a more permanent impression. We are certainly living in an age that requires work to catch the eye, when ideas and products are forever competing for our attention.

Technology has become central to our lives. Whereas a few years ago the activities of the graphic designer were mainly restricted to the creation of posters, advertisements, packaging, signs etc, the modern designer's work has now expanded to embrace virtually every field of representation and design.

Paper has been replaced in part by digital screens, extending advertising space from static to animation. Meanwhile, fonts are no longer listed to a single colour, they can animate, while variable fonts allow custom styles to be generated from a single font file. All of this has resulted, from a brand perspective, in visual identities that have transformed from the static to dynamic, with much richer possibilities of communication than were previously afforded.

The visual landscape which today's designers are contributing to is very cluttered and the digital world alone is so vast that sometimes it feels hard to make your voice heard amongst all the noise. We're surrounded by messaging, which is progressively coming in the form of digital advertising; whether that's from the phone in our pocket, digital billboards, tablets or desktop screens. However, this messaging usually comes without audio, so to communicate, typographically can be key.

This is perhaps why, as seen in this book, we see so many brand identities, advertising and digital designs that have a typographic emphasis today. They lead with type, they play with and subtly animate type or celebrate type's inherent beauty by putting it centre stage within their designs. These are designs with a strength and conviction intended to cut through the visual noise we encounter everyday and communicate a message, elicit a response or represent a call to action.

This is achieved through the use of core principles of graphic design such as scale, repetition, dominance and emphasis which can affect the meaning, tone and entire composition of a design.

They are responsible for creating a visual hierarchy among elements in graphic design and can help inform an audience which elements to look at, in what order to look at them and what is most important to focus on. They can help tell a story, create a visual journey, portray rhythm and movement, consider similarities, or even shift perspective and playfully create whimsical or surreal scenes.

The work on show within this book represents an important and fascinating direction in typographic design. I'm excited to see where this collision of technology, typography and trends will take us in the future.

It's been an immense pleasure to take a look at the next wave of innovation in typographic design and examine how designers can produce work that stands out. Lastly, it goes without saying that, for a book such as this, we're obviously deeply indebted to all of those who have contributed work to *Big Type* and agreed to be interviewed. We thank you all for your time, support and talent.

**Jon Dowling**: Counter-Print

# SCALE

*Contributing Designers:* Order • Principal • Futura • Playtype • Ragged Edge INTERVIEW • PORTO ROCHA • Astrid Stavro – Pentagram • Accompany • Design by Toko • Studio de Ronners • Pràctica • Jens Nilsson • Han Gao • Campbell Hay →

# Elkin

**Order / order.design**
🌐 USA

Elkin Editions is an independent video production studio based in New York City. Order developed a new moniker for the company, 'Elkin', as a way to quickly identify the company amidst the often similar-looking production environments.

# Amphithéâtre de Trois-Rivières

Principal / principal.studio
⊕ Canada

At the confluence of the Saint-Maurice and Saint-Lawrence Rivers, the Amphithéâtre de Trois-Rivières is a highlight of the Mauricie territory. The building, conceived by Paul Laurendau, won the *Governor General's Award* in architecture. Principal was given the mandate to work on identificatory interventions associated with the venue's spatial markings and to conceive a functional signage for the new building.

The signage project was developed to fit directly into the architecture in such a way as to reduce the need for physical props. Walls and doors become informative spaces. A series of pictograms was created to clarify the signage itinerary. The outcome was an elegant clarity of messaging highlighted by the architecture. The simplicity of the system and its typographical refinement are now characteristic of the venue.

Scale

# BLOP

Futura / byfutura.com
🌐 Australia

*BLOP* is an art, design and culture festival that was streamed digitally for two days in December 2020. Presented by Fondeadora and curated by Futura, *BLOP* showcased 13 highly influential creatives based in Mexico City, Buenos Aires and Barcelona that led them through the lens of various disciplines: design, art, gastronomy, illustration and new technologies.

   *BLOP* was born from the idea of breaking the 'bubble' that isolated us all during Covid's lockdown; to break that barrier through culture, uniting creatives with new ways of perception. Based on this concept, Futura developed the branding for the entire festival with images of balloons inflating to the point of breaking. Likewise, a rich and varied typeface was designed with alternative characters.

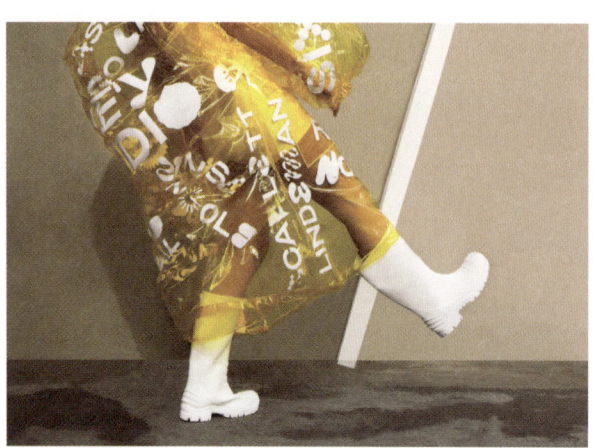

# Scale

Big Type

# TypePlay
# By Playtype

**Playtype / playtype.com**
⊕ **Denmark**

As a continuing series Playtype are inviting designers and visual artists from around the world to contribute designs for their courtyard billboard.

No creative restrictions — simply a format and a typeface.

The aim of this project is to highlight upcoming, as well as established designers, studios and visual artists and invite the contributors to use the billboard as a visual playground.

**Featured designers:**
Paul Bergès - France
Two Times Elliot - UK
Marina Veziko - Finland
Studio Blackburn - UK
Sarah Boris - UK
Tobias Hönow - Germany
Tobias Røder - Denmark

18

Buchstaben
aneinandergereiht
zu Wörtern
in einer anderen Sprache
geschrieben
auf einer Wand
in Kopenhagen

IT DON'T MATTER IF YOU'RE BLACK OR LIGHT

# INTERVIEW
## Ragged Edge / Chris Clayton

raggededge.com
🌐 UK

Reveal

Ragged Edge is a branding agency for people who, 'care less about how things are, and more about how things could be'. They call them 'Changemakers'. Ragged Edge's process is designed to reward bravery — taking their clients to the edge of what's possible and creating brands that can drive meaningful change.

**What is your background and how did you become involved in graphic design?**

I actually never wanted to go to University. I wanted to play football. However, I had a really inspirational tutor at the London College of Communication and he knew how to motivate me, and how to get the best work out of me. He told me about the legendary graphic design course at St Martins and encouraged me to apply. He explained that if you're lucky enough to get a place then St Martins isn't an opportunity you turn down. I was offered a place at St Martins in 2003, and the rest is history. And so was my dream of becoming a professional footballer.

After I graduated I spent six months as an Art Director at an advertising agency. But I realised advertising wasn't for me. I decided branding was more interesting, and the idea of a smaller agency really appealed. Somewhere I could have an impact as a Junior. I found the ideal boutique branding agency where I stayed for eight years, where I became their Design Director. Practicing and fine tuning the art of branding along the way, working closely with the clients and founders. Our clients ranged from international art fairs to the Four Seasons hotels.

I left the boutique branding world to freelance, see how different agencies operated and look for opportunities to work on more ambitious projects. And that's how I ended up at Ragged Edge.

**How would you describe your creative style and process?**

I would describe my creative process as open and curious. I always love how ideas form and change along the journey. Whatever we create over the course of the process is always so different to what I first might have imagined. It's important to remain open minded throughout so you can let new ideas form, even when timings are tight and pressure is mounting.

I would love to describe my creative style as effortless, simple, concise and bold. With a strong idea at the heart of it. If the idea is simple enough to be easily understood and shines a new light on a truth that everyone can relate to, then everything should flow from there. A strong, single minded idea can make the work feel effortless, like it was all meant to be this way, and it couldn't be anything else.

**Typography has a strong prominence in your portfolio. Why is type so important to your work?**

Typography is the visual thread that runs through a brand, it's the absolute constant on every piece of communication. So the signals sent — even if they are received subconsciously — need to be carefully judged because it will affect how your audience perceives

# Scale

your brand. It can make a message seem strong or soft. Or make you believe a product or service is premium or accessible. It's a powerful asset that every brand should be using to its fullest. And when you pair powerful typography with incredible writing, then the results are greater than the sum of its parts.

### How would you define good typography?
There's a famous modernist principle that says 'good typography is invisible'. While I agree with its original intention, and it is certainly a principle we use in digital product design to reduce cognitive loads and improve user experience, when it comes to branding, I now believe the opposite to be true; good typography is distinctive, memorable and makes you feel something.

### Do you have a favourite font and why?
*Noe Display* by Schick Toikka is probably my favourite font at the moment. It's inspired by traditional Latin forms, so it feels familiar. But it's acute triangular wedge serifs, high x-height and vertical stress all makes it feel modern, unapologetically bold and perfect for a whole range of applications.

### How can effective design enhance a brand's identity?
Changing people's behaviour is the hardest thing to achieve for a brand because you can't rely on a rational argument. Despite the fact that many people rationalise decisions after the fact, emotion drives the initial choice. People are inherently emotional, so if they want to change minds, they need to win hearts first. Brands need to define the emotional response they want to generate from their audience.

And design, along with writing, is the key to achieving that goal.

### In a world in which we are spending so much time online, bombarded by messaging, is there a greater need for simpler, more direct identity design?
Absolutely. We live in the attention age. The world is getting noisier. Information is coming thicker and faster. And methods for commandeering our attention are becoming more and more sophisticated. There is already a trend towards simpler and more direct identity design and product designers are always trying to reduce cognitive loads. Ultimately though, we have to stop thumbs from scrolling, catch eye balls, win hearts and convince minds. So simple and direct is a really great way to cut through the noise. But simplicity isn't enough. Your brand needs to stand out, it needs to stand for something different, not just better. So if you can combine simplicity with distinctiveness, then you have a chance of getting noticed and then being remembered.

### What is your studio driven by creatively?
We're driven by the challenge in front of us. We always want each project to be better than the last but we have learned to leave our egos at the door. Our creative goal is to create something new, unique, distinctive and memorable. That journey starts by creating a strategic leap and taking the client somewhere they'd never considered before. A leap that defines the client's position as different, not just better. This strategic approach then inspires how we express the brand we're creating visually and verbally. We don't have a house style and believe that everything should be driven by the concept. And that concept needs to be simple

enough to be easily understood, but rich enough to flex across the whole brand.

### What do you think of the design scene in London today? How has it evolved?
The London design scene has changed a lot since I graduated. It just keeps getting better and better. There's an endless number of hugely talented boutique studios, and the largest studios are relentless champions of creativity. The culture of the London design scene is one that encourages a progressive,

Big Type

East London Liquor Co.

growth mindset and as a result, we're seeing some of the best work in the world. In terms of the concentration of quality, diversity and richness, I think that London is the most exciting design scene in the world.

**What are your goals for the future of Ragged Edge?**
We're a branding agency for people who care less about how things are and more about how they could be. We work with clients trying to define what the world could be. And in turn, change the world.

Scale

# Otta

**Ragged Edge / raggededge.com**
🌐 UK

Finding a job is an outdated system of endless trawling, irrelevant ads and faceless recruiters treating candidates like commodities. Otta shook things up with a candidate-first career platform that brings the best out of people in a way a CV never could, and in return, brings them only the best roles from only the best companies.

The brand is rich and expressive, the antithesis of a corporate jobs platform, starting with a logo designed to stand apart — just like Otta's candidates. Together with an unapologetic typeface that works with messaging to get straight to the point, the Otta brand is a job well done.

Scale

# Museu Nacional

**PORTO ROCHA** / portorocha.com
🌐 USA

Museu Nacional da República is the largest public art museum in Brasília, known for its modernist dome designed by renowned architect Oscar Niemeyer.

To help strengthen the relationship between the institution and its public, PORTO ROCHA crafted a new visual identity for Museu. Balancing utilitarian, modernist rigour with an inviting tone of voice creates a uniquely Brazilian visual language, referencing both the country's contributions to modern architecture and the warm energy of its people. Typographically, *Founders Grotesk* recalls the visual language of Brasília's early urban development, with circular letterforms that allude to the shape of Museu's iconic dome.

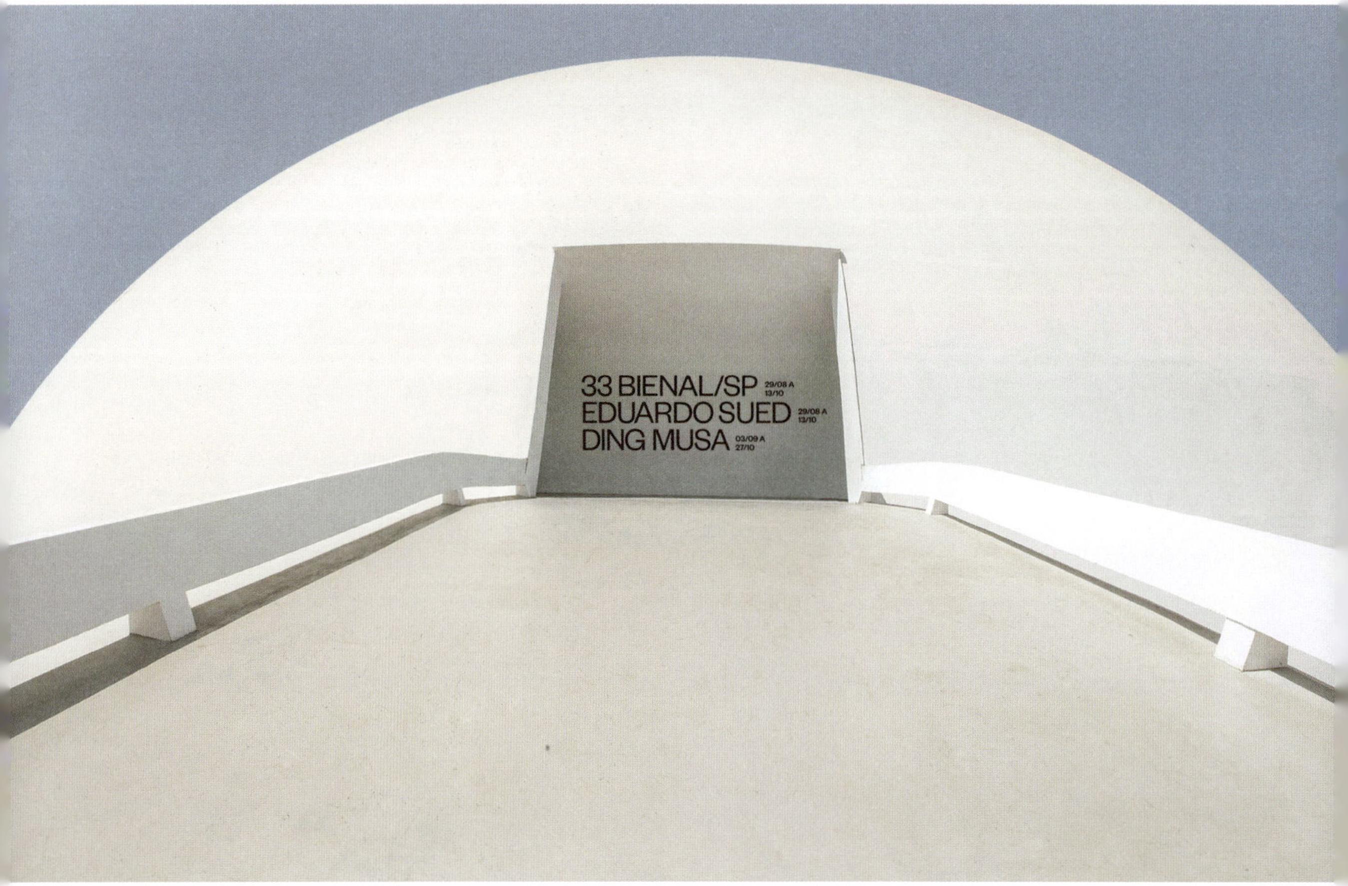

Big Type

Big Type

29

Scale

# National Ambulance Mental Health Group

**Astrid Stavro – Pentagram / pentagram.com**
⊕ UK

The National Ambulance Mental Health Group (NAMHG) represents ambulance trusts in England and promotes best practice in pre-hospital mental health care. Astrid Stavro's new identity is designed to work across all platforms and sizes, from social media icons to large-scale environmental graphics. The monogram depicts a person in pictogram form – the blue circle represents their head and mind, and references the blue lights used by ambulances. When used on its own, the monogram references the harmony needed between mind and body, and when repeated, it represents community and becomes a graphic element which can be used to visualise infographics.

Scale

# Merino

**Accompany / accompany.group**
🌐 Australia

Merino is a family-owned business offering two distinct services of construction and building consultancy. Brand and design practice Accompany, established that the greatest impact for the business would be to create a base visual language shared across the two services with considered points of visual distinction between them. The system revolves around an adaptable 'M' icon that changes its form and colour between the two offerings. *Ivar Display Condensed,* used for headlines and body-copy, creates a high contrast to the neutral appearance of the wordmark set in *Atlas Grotesk*. The typography is key in forming an identity that represents Merino's can-do meets craftsmanship approach.

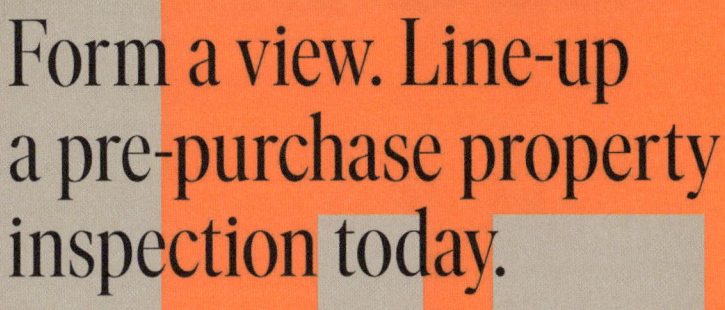

Scale

# White Rabbit Gallery

**Design by Toko / designbytoko.com**
🌐 **The Netherlands / Australia**

The White Rabbit Gallery is a contemporary art museum located in the inner city Sydney suburb of Chippendale, Australia and owns one of the world's most significant collections of Chinese contemporary art.

This publication, just like the comprehensive collection, is the sum of its parts. 99 different clamshell boxes house three books, each executed in 99 cover variations. With the total number of box sets limited to 2475, none are identical.

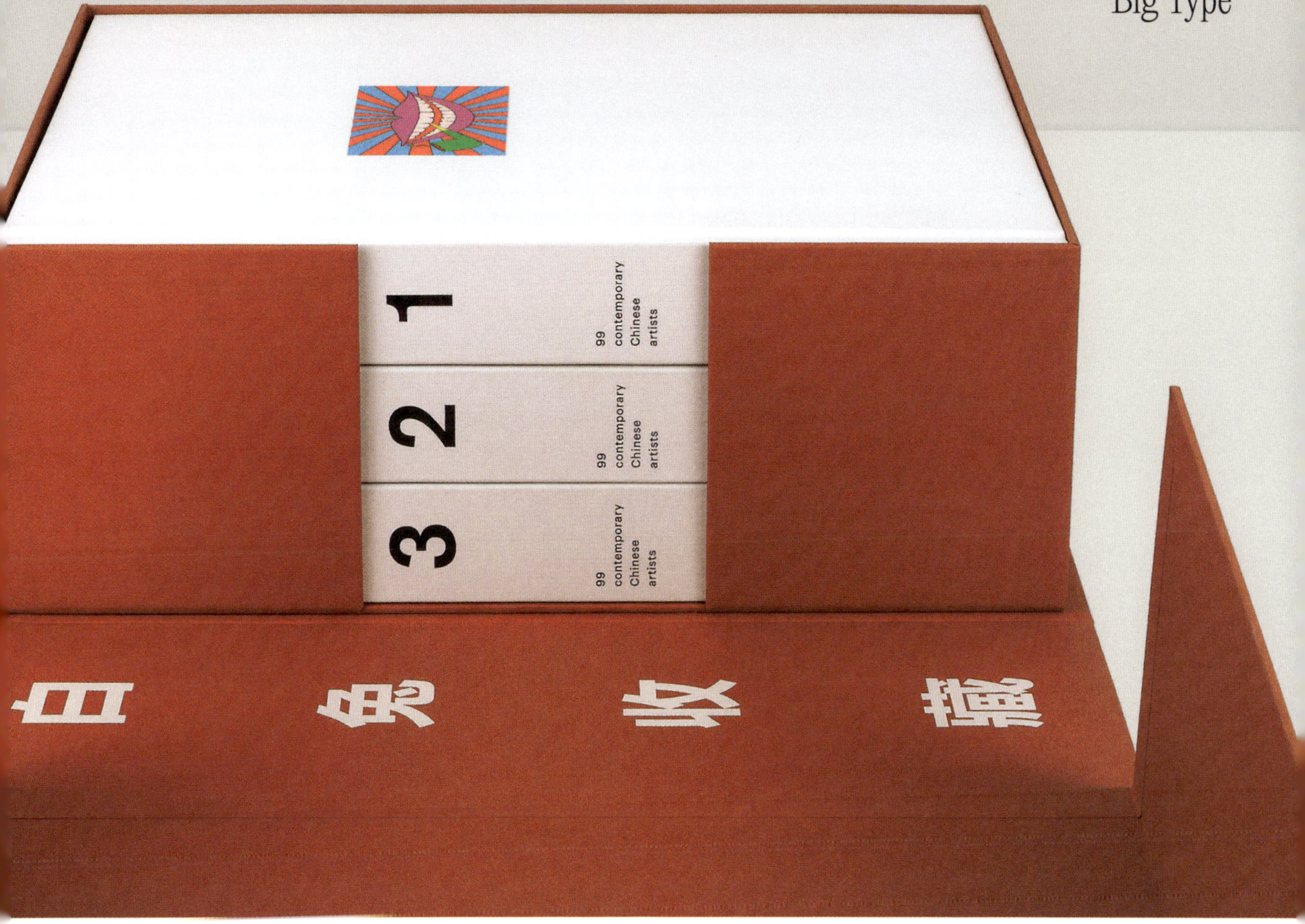

Big Type

Scale

# My Sister is a Martian

Design by Toko / designbytoko.com
🌐 The Netherlands / Australia

This redesign of the book *My Sister is a Martian*, was written by Beau Neilson, daughter of White Rabbit Gallery owner Judith Neilson, when she was just nine years old. It features multi-coloured boxes, screen printed on all sides.

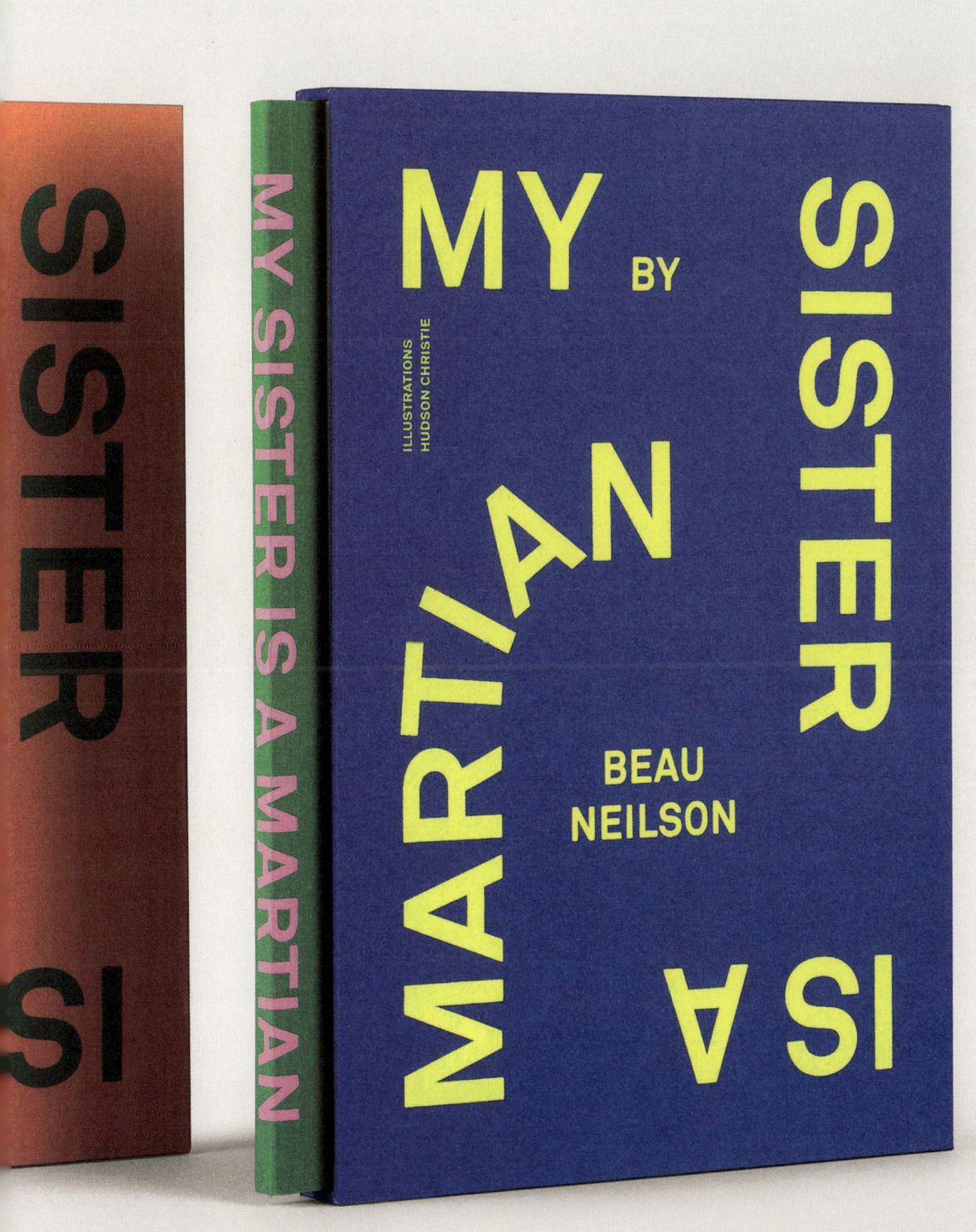

Scale

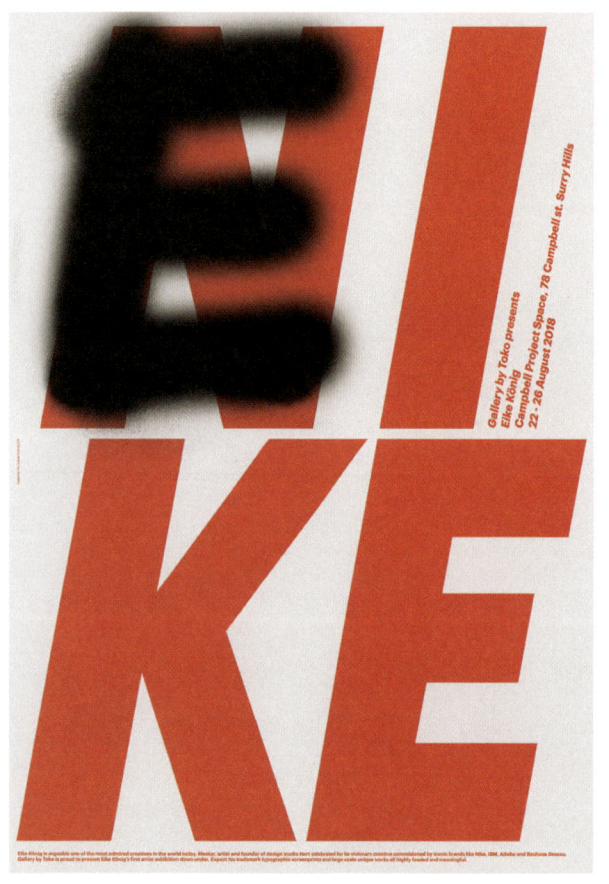 

## Gallery by Toko

Design by Toko / designbytoko.com
🌐 The Netherlands / Australia
This poster for an Eike König exhibition was created as a limited edition screen print on a heavy stock, with the 'E' applied by hand.

## Nieuwe Bossche School

Design by Toko / designbytoko.com
🌐 The Netherlands / Australia
This poster submission was for *Algemene Beschouwingen* (election posters that matter). Design by Toko's submission is based on the iconography of Dutch voting ballets. With populism on the rise their hope was that voters would stay optimistic (considering current difficult times) and opt wisely during elections.

## Figures Exhibition

Design by Toko / designbytoko.com
🌐 The Netherlands / Australia
Poster for the *Figures* exhibition at Australia Council for the Arts, based on Design by Toko's exhibition design.

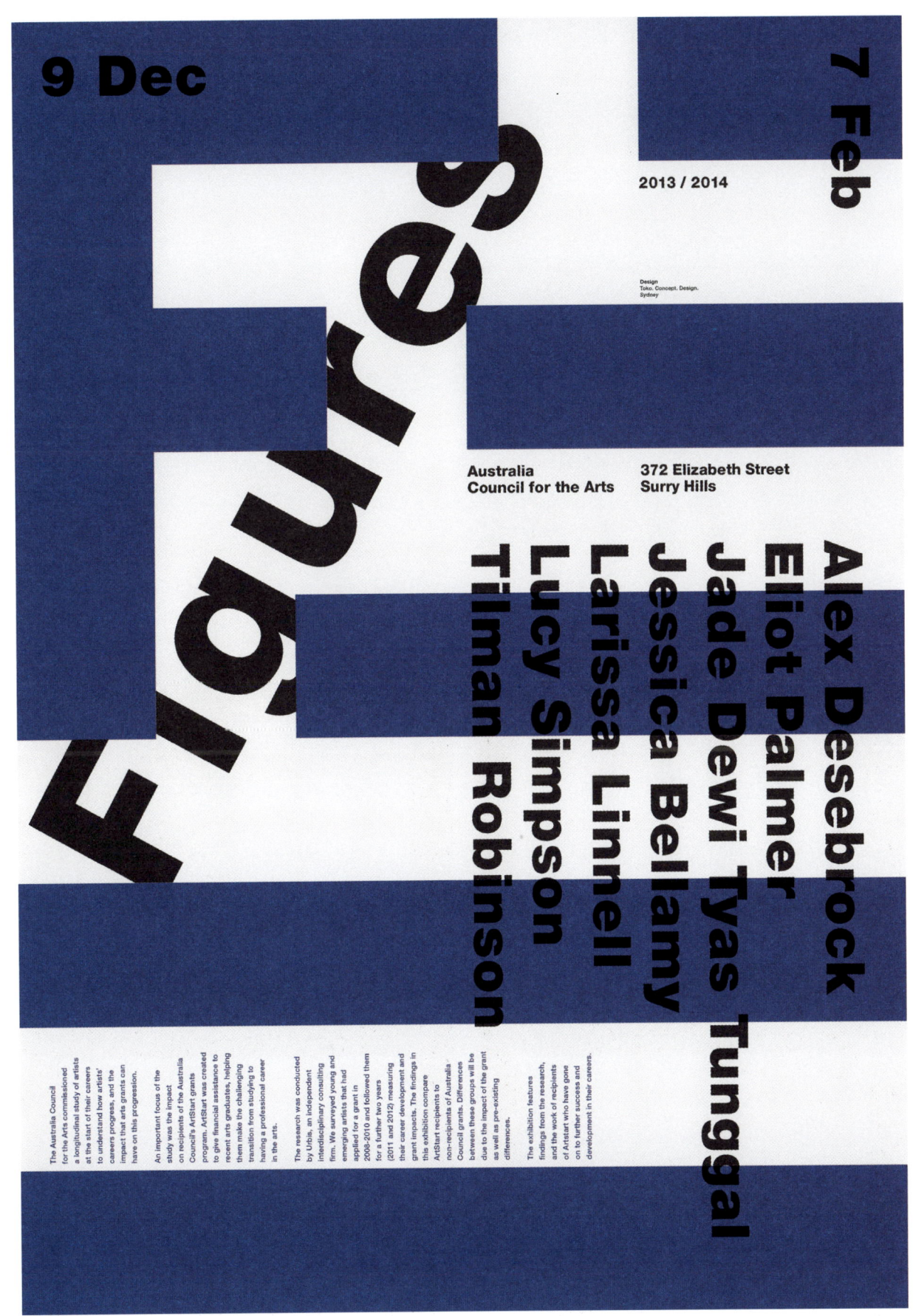

# Jardins de Métis

Principal / principal.studio
🌐 Canada

Located at the mouth of the Mitis river in the Gaspé, the *Jardins de Métis* were created at the very start of the last century. These horticultural gardens, open to the public for the last fifty years, are now a major tourist attraction for the region.

To augment the gardens' creative and tourist offerings, a large open space was set up in which, every year, creators from around the world are invited to create contemporary garden projects.

Principal produced and illustrated the festival campaign for several years. A firmly contemporary visual direction was adopted, highlighting the creative and experimental approach of interventions produced on the site, while also making sure the message reached the very wide audience that visited the gardens.

The visual approach to this edition reflected the theme of the event: *Terrains de Jeux* (playground). The poster's composition employed a colourful and playful interplay of formal and typographic elements, which all seem to be moving while striving to maintain balance. The promotional campaign was composed of a poster, a program, and various publications on digital platforms.

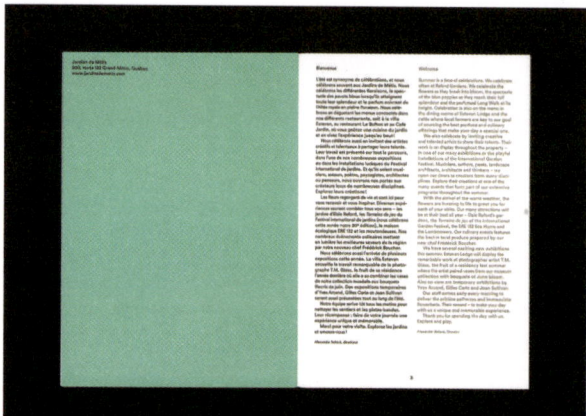
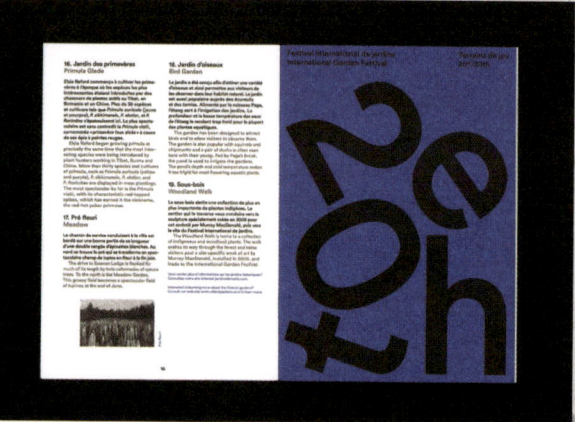
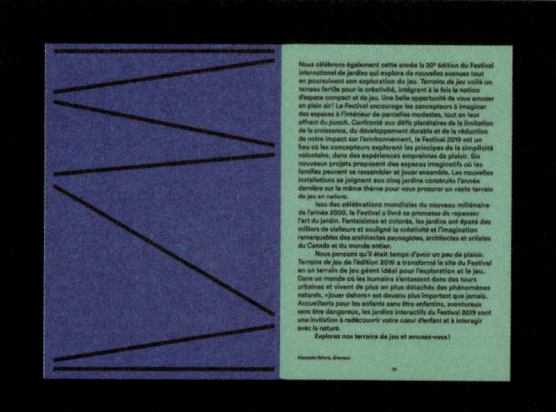
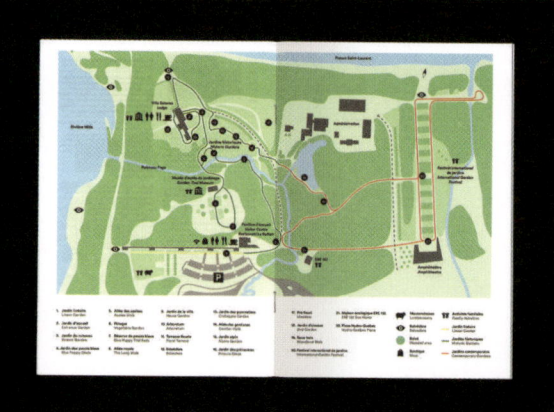

Scale

# BNO

**Studio de Ronners / deronners.nl**
⊕ **The Netherlands**

BNO (Association of Dutch Designers) has stood up for designers' rights for over a century. Despite being the largest community of designers and design agencies in The Netherlands, too many people are unfamiliar with their practice. Studio de Ronners was commissioned to enlarge their brand awareness. They started with a promotional campaign at the *Dutch Design Week,* the largest design event in Northern Europe with more than 355,000 visitors. Studio de Ronners designed a flyer series targeting the most critical audience imaginable: designers. Therefore, they came up with bold statements about the BNO such as 'Your coach to success' and 'Shitload of good contracts' placed on brightly coloured flyers, turning ordinary flyers into design objects. With 'Made by Dutch Designers' – the main statement – they framed the BNO in just four words. Join BNO, because we are Dutch Designers just like you.

43

Scale

We fight for your rights.

Yes, join BNC

Shitload of good contracts.

Yes, join BNC

Your c to suc

Yes, jo BN

Big Type

45

# Irvington Theater

Pràctica / practica.design
🌐 Spain

First opened in 1902, Irvington Theater has become a cultural heart of the Hudson Rivertowns, in New York. In 2019 the Theater Commission built new ambitions for their programming. The aim became to showcase the diverse range and wealth of events produced by the theater and their arts partners, and revitalise and centralise their brand identity in a way that could be produced by their newly assembled internal team.

The brand identity is designed to capture the cultural energy flowing through the theater: inspired by the visual language of old-school advertisement and wheatpaste posters, Pràctica created a system based on two main elements — layering and vernacular typography.

Layering is a metaphor of the passage of time, achieved both through stacking and colour. The wood-inspired typography captures the vibrance of the varied cultural personalities passing through the Irvington Theater.

Finally, they simplified the naming from Irvington Town Hall Theater to Irvington Theater, which is more direct and memorable.

Creative Direction & Graphic Design: Pràctica & Andrea Trabucco.

SUPER-NATURAL

LEGEND OF

CALEB TEICHER

TWELFTH NIGHT

THEN TAKE ACTION

TREE

ANDY PITZ

JOCELYN & CHRIS

TWO-HUNDRED

ON THE HUDSON
SLEEPY HO
& NYC GARE
NYC COMEDY
THE LAVEND
OF LIFE
ARWAA
ARNDT CONCER

Scale     Aight

Jens Nilsson /
jens-nilsson.com
⊕ Sweden

This type treatment and label design was created by Jens Nilsson for PangPang's beer *Aight* — a light, refreshing and crisp lager made for American summer nights.

# NICE CREAM

Han Gao / behance.net/han-gao
⊕ China

This logo, brand and packaging design for *NICE CREAM*, a low-calorie healthy ice cream, was Han Gao's attempt to re-examine the food industry's design style, of using pictures in a regular way, and injecting vitality into it. The design of the packaging captures the habits of healthy food users, highlights the nutritional elements and has helped shape a new generation of ice cream brands, through the reorganisation of information levels and bright colours.

# IQL

**Campbell Hay / campbellhay.com**
🌐 UK

International Quarter London, as it was formerly known, is a forward-thinking new property development situated next to the Olympic Park in London. Its bold ambition to create the workplace of the future required an expressive visual identity and an impactful placemaking programme to match.

Rebranding the development to IQL — a clearer, shorter, more memorable moniker — Campbell Hay created a modular visual system inspired by large architectural forms. Contemporary, graphic and playful, each shape could be adapted to express an idea or a behaviour, allowing IQL to manifest physical 'moments' on-site, and establishing a sense of anticipation and participation within the community.

# REPEAT

*Contributing Designers:* PORTO ROCHA INTERVIEW
• Husmee • Brand Brothers • Lukas Diemling • Seachange →

# INTERVIEW
## PORTO ROCHA / Leo Porto & Felipe Rocha

portorocha.com
🌐 USA

**Melissa Flygrl.** Photography: Mari Juliano / Leonardo Sang.

PORTO ROCHA is a New York-based design studio developing creative and strategic work that engages deeply with the world we live in. Working closely with people and companies to craft branding systems, products and experiences, they seek to provoke meaningful change through their work, from large-scale projects that reach significant audiences to socially and culturally-motivated initiatives.

## What are your backgrounds and how did you become involved in graphic design?

<sup>LP</sup> I've been interested in design since I was very young. I used to design flyers, birthday invitations and posters for friends as a hobby, but it took me a long time to realise I could pursue it as a professional career. I eventually enrolled at SVA in New York to study advertising, and after realising it wasn't exactly what I wanted to do, I switched to graphic design. Four years later, having graduated from SVA and having had the opportunity to work and learn from many inspiring people, staying in New York and continuing my career here felt like a natural move. I worked at Chermayeff&Geismar&Haviv, Pentagram and COLLINS. 10 years later, I have my own design studio with my partner, Felipe Rocha.

<sup>FR</sup> I did a technical course in graphic design during high school and got my first design job at 17, which is very common in Brazil, especially for people who can't afford to pay for college but need to find a vocation. I worked in advertising for a few years and opened a small design studio with my friends in parallel. In 2012 I got a scholarship at Fabrica (Benetton's creative lab in Italy), learned a lot there, and came back to Brazil to finish my Bachelor's degree a year later. When I finally graduated from college, I had no concrete plans to move abroad again; But one day I randomly sent an email to Jessica Walsh asking for a job, and it just worked out.

## How would you describe your creative style and process?

Formally speaking, it's hard to describe our style because we believe in approaching each project differently, considering our client's unique contexts and audiences. We try to avoid leaning on visual trends, and always pressure-test solutions with the, 'how will this look in 5 years, 10 years?', question. You could also say that our style is pretty type-driven.

↑ **Samba.** Photography: Mari Juliano.
**Electric Sky.** Photography: Luca Venter / Corey Olsen.

↑ *You Were Born For This: Astrology for Radical Self Acceptance,* published by Harper Collins. Photography: Mari Juliano / Nick-Wons.
**Live.** Photography: Coletivo Amapoa.
↗ **Bonde.** Photography: Hick Duarte / Mari Juliano.

**Typography has a strong prominence in your portfolio. Why is type so important to your work?**

Typography is extremely important to us because it is the vehicle for expressing language and giving a soul and intention to words. The choice of typography can drastically change the tone of voice, so choosing the right typeface and font makes all the difference. It is also extremely nuanced (all the details from scale and weight down to the minutiae of tracking, leading, etc. need to be considered). Of course, typography also carries cultural and historical baggage – the subtle and sometimes not-so-subtle symbolic connotations of type are something we're always navigating.

**How would you define good typography?**

From a technical perspective, good typography means that kerning, line-spacing, ragging, etc. were considered. But besides being technical, we believe that typography is good when it is tailored to its context, regardless of the font style.

**Do you have a favourite font and why?**
We always have a hard time answering this question and the answer is always the same. We don't have a favorite font. We do have a couple of type foundries that we love and whose work we follow. Dinamo, Commercial Type, and Radim Pesko are probably our favorites.

**What do you think of the design scene in New York today?**
New York is a very competitive city and it can be very tough and even unhealthy to live and work here. But as immigrants ourselves, the aspect that we love about NY is its diversity and multiculturalism. We love meeting designers from all over the world that are passionate about their work and want to build new things in this city — this is probably the most special thing about the design scene in NY.

**What is your studio driven by creatively?**
Our studio is driven by the idea that we can help people and brands express themselves more intentionally, to help define and shape their purpose in the world, to add value to the experiences they offer and to pave their path for a brighter future.

**What are your goals for Porto Rocha over the coming years?**
We want to continue growing the studio in a sustainable way and create design work that is memorable and relevant today and hopefully tomorrow. We also hope that the studio can help to promote diversity in the design world.

# Melissa Flygrl

**PORTO ROCHA** / portorocha.com
🌐 USA

In 2017, the well-known Brazilian shoe brand Melissa launched the highly anticipated *Flygrl* collection with a progressive campaign that encouraged all girls and women to 'fly with freedom'. The visual language vitalises this sense of liberation by juxtaposing elements that do not typically belong together, creating a sense of tension that permeates all aspects of the campaign including e-commerce, social media, retail, and editorial. Inspired by the typographic vernacular of protest posters, *Druk Condensed* was used to create an expressive yet intuitive type-layout system, allowing for both impactful headlines and widespread flexibility as the design was implemented across Melissa's global markets.

# Kunsthal 2019

HUSMEE / husmee.com
🌐 Spain

This campaign was for Bilbao, where the Kunsthal design school were opening new headquarters. The key was presenting the school to the city – a 'Hello' to Bilbao, to design, to culture, to the future.

The composition of the posters follow the structure born through the corporate grid, and typographical messages are placed on top of white modules that symbolise adhesive tapes.

63

# FUTURE

Centro Superior de Diseño
Goi Mailako Diseinu Zentroa
Kunsthal.es

# KUNSTHAL

# DESIGN

# FUTURE
# FUTURE
# FUTURE
# FUTURE
# FUTURE
# FUTURE

**Estudios Superiores de Diseño. Matrícula abierta.**

**Goi Mailako Disenu Ikasketak. Matrikula irekia.**

**Kunsthal, future is design.**

20 años formando profesionales del diseño, ahora en Bilbao.

20 urtez diseinatzaileak hezitzen. Orain Bilbon.

# Baehl

### Brand Brothers / brandbrothers.fr
🌐 France

Baehl defines itself as a European strategic healthcare boutique providing services in innovation strategy, market entry, clinical adoption and market launch. Based in Paris but operating across many countries, they work on the most advanced issues related to innovation for health, offer integrated services and cover the complete lifecycle of a product or business. Baehl is a team of senior innovators, strategists, scientists, medical doctors and market explorers who together help build the future of healthcare across all sectors of the life sciences industry.

Brand Brothers was commissioned to redefine the company's graphic identity. They opted for a sleek but structured typographic design, custom-made for the occasion, whose lines subtly evoke a dynamic of growth and forward projection. Based on the curves of the 'B', they developed a generative pattern, used in black monochrome or coupled with experimental textures reminiscent of the world of research and life sciences. This rich and organic texture is complemented by minimalistic and structured print and web collaterals, based on *Labil Grotesk* (Kometa).

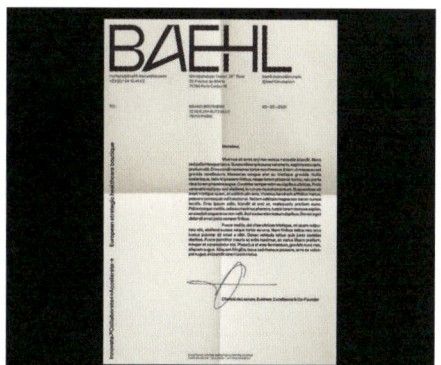

Repeat

# Bens Bier

Lukas Diemling / diemling.com
⊕ Austria

With the utmost care and an unconventional fresh approach Bens Bier founder Ben Seidel creates excellent beers in collaboration with local brewers. Ben reached out to Lukas Diemling to create a visual identity and package design which differs from the competition and introduces the brand to the audience with a clear message, 'it is all about Ben and his Beer'.

A custom logotype with a strong and individual appearance communicates the straight forward, unconventional approach of Bens Bier. The logotype is applied edge to edge to underline their message on all applications and is supported by Klim Type's *Founders Grotesk Condensed*.

Repeat

## Oji Sushi

**Seachange / seachange.studio**
🌐 New Zealand

Oji is a new takeaway sushi experience in New Zealand — a country where sushi is the most popular lunch food.

    The brief was to create a fun and memorable brand that stood out in a sea of mundane and familiar sushi vendors. Oji translates as 'Uncle', and Seachange took this as inspiration to create an iconic sushi character. His eyes are drawn to represent the fillings in sushi, and resemble the Japanese flag from the top. Oji's simplicity of form allows him to take the shape of a sushi roll, bend and dance, grow and morph, get cut up, and wink.

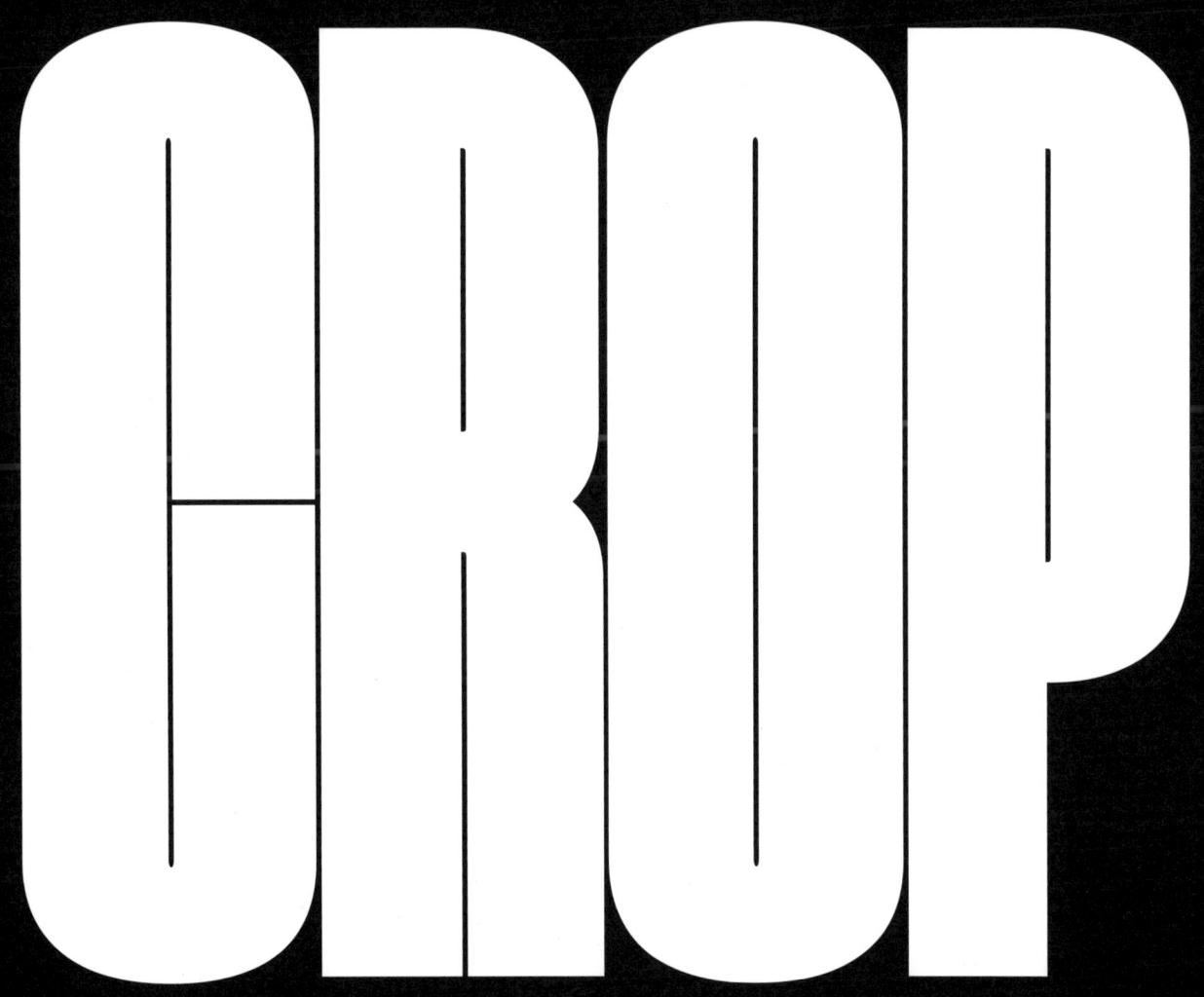

*Contributing Designers:* Anthony Burrill • Jens Nilsson • Caserne INTERVIEW • Studio de Ronners • Forth + Back • Marisa Piñana • North • Principal • Pràctica →

Crop

Big Type

# YOU&ME and ME&YOU

Anthony Burrill / anthonyburrill.com
⊕ UK

This largescale public artwork in the historic centre of Leeds, West Yorkshire, acted as a message of unity for 2021. Curated by Laura Wellington at In Good Company, it was supported by King & Co and installed by Bread Collective.

**Photography**: Chris Spencer-Payne.

Big Type

Big Type

# Packhelp

**Jens Nilsson / jens-nilsson.com**
🌐 Sweden

This series of typographic mailer boxes was designed for Packhelp's launch on the Swedish market. Each side of the packaging builds up of the word 'Help'.

# INTERVIEW
## Caserne / Léo Breton-Allaire

caserne.com
🌐 Canada

*Love Is the Message, the Message Is Death* at the Montreal Museum of Contemporary Art (MAC)

Caserne are an independent full-service design studio. Their approach is distinguished by their relevant concepts, but above all by their desire to build iconic brands. The brands they create attain their uniqueness by the strength of their stories and their missions.

### What are your backgrounds and how did you become involved in graphic design?

At an early age and without knowing each other, both of us (Ugo Varin-Lachapelle and Léo Breton-Allaire) had similar interests in marginal sports and culture such as skateboarding and skiing. Both sports presented at the time, and even more so today, environments in which graphic design was prominent. Following theses hobbies, we were introduced to 'multimedia' by filming or taking pictures of ourselves and our friends in our respective sports. Both of us developed a strong interest in branding and visual communication in a broader way, and then we met at UQAM university, both studying at the graphic design school in 2012. From there we followed a classic graphic design path.

### How would you describe your creative style and process?

There is not really one style that can define all of our work, each project is unique, we enjoy re-inventing ourselves with each design exercise and staying away from repetitive mechanics.

We value the contribution of strategy in a brand design exercise to ensure that the project meets the desired and expected success beyond (and in addition to) having good graphic qualities. Caserne is a strategic design studio. We make sure to shake the status quo.

### Typography has a strong prominence in your portfolio. Why is type so important to your work?

Both of us had similar interests at a young age, without knowing each other, for marginal sports such as skateboarding and we love to play with that. Copywriting itself is also an important part of our work, through which we find a lot of opportunities to express a brand. Whether it's a design exercise or branding work, the choice of typography and its customisation is one of the major step in our projects. We were lucky enough to share our offices with the typographic foundry Coppers and Brasses for three years. We already had a strong interest in typography and I think this move just pushed us even harder in that direction. To this day we still continue to work with them on projects where we feel custom-designed fonts would be a relevant addition to the exercise.

### How would you define good typography?

The first basis of a good typeface is the drawing itself, including the kerning and the strength of the overall font family. As designers, we believe that the key lies in the use and the relevance we give to the typography in a platform. Good or not so good, it depends mainly on the use and the choice to use it in different contexts of a graphic platform.

### Do you have a favourite font and why?

Absolutely and I would say that our natural choices and studies of typefaces are directed by foundries and not by typefaces directly: Commercial Type, Optimo, Dinamo, Colophon, Production Type, Coppers and Brasses and Lineto. We know that from credible and experienced foundries, we will find a quality product that will meet our needs.

### How often is typography used as the starting point for your design work?

Once the direction, territory or message is identified, typography is always the starting point for design exercises at the studio. It is around this choice that the other parameters will revolve.

↑ Nightlife by Cyprien Gaillard at the Montreal Museum of Contemporary Art (MAC)
Club Kombucha
2020 Montreal International Documentary Festival

# Crop

> The team shares a common vision, that of leading world-class, unique and tailor-made projects with a marked relevance to our clients' industry and also to our business sector.

**How can effective design enhance a brand's identity?**
Design definitely contributes to the success of brands. A good platform combines the tools to enhance the functional aspect on the one hand, but also other tools or mechanics that allow to create emotions in all public communication contexts. Design allows clear and unique communications.

**What are your main goals and considerations when working on the design of beverage identities and their labelling?**
There are a lot of considerations in packaging, but I think what we're looking for the most is that it stands out on a shelf. In packaging once you're visible you've already done a big part of your design job. That said, standing out means really different things depending on the product category or the context in which the product will exist. When we think about standing out, the usual reflex is to think about truly visible colours (fluro for example), but in some contexts sobriety can also be really key to create breaks in the tablet space. A good example is Silo. The brewery/microbrewery category in Quebec is so saturated with illustration and colours that we decided to be as pure as possible to create this disruption.

**What do you think of the design scene in Montreal today? How has it evolved?**
The Montreal scene is super-active right now. It's effervescent and really of a remarkable quality. There are a lot of design studios in Montreal that are making their mark internationally. I seriously think we have one of the strongest scenes right now.

We owe a lot of that to the pioneering Montreal studios that opened the doors and the space for human scale studios. Studios like Paprika, Feed, Uniforme (now Principal) that have been showing people of our generation for over 20 years that there was a place in the market for studios founded and operated by graphic designers.

**What is your studio driven by creatively?**
The team shares a common vision, that of leading world-class, unique and tailor-made projects with a marked relevance to our clients' industry and also to our business sector. Once the vision is established, it is the individuality of the designers, their personal interests or backgrounds, whether in art, music, sports, fashion, or all of these put together that creates value in all our projects.

↑ Brasserie Caserne
← Silo
→ Cidres Polisson
　RÉUNION

Crop

# Love Is the Message, the Message Is Death

# Arthur Jafa — MAC

Caserne / caserne.com
🌐 Canada

The MAC presented a striking artwork-event by artist and filmmaker Arthur Jafa, *Love Is the Message, the Message Is Death, 2016,* a rapid-fire montage of images from a mesmerising range of sources. The work grew out of the recognition of the widespread circulation of images of the abuse of black bodies on YouTube. At once a celebration of black creativity and excellence, and a depiction of the violence of the state, this immersive projection presented powerful and devastating manifestations of physical restraint and liberation.

The visuals developed play with positive and negative space as an interpretation of both the beauty and madness of the topics addressed in the artwork. The bold typography is also a reminder of manifestation, since the character design was inspired by protest signs.

**Photography:** François Ollivier.

Big Type

## Let's Get Physical

### Studio de Ronners / deronners.nl
### ⊕ The Netherlands

*Let's Get Physical* was a sculpture route by AVL Mundo throughout the area of West-Rotterdam. AVL Mundo is a non-profit organisation founded by Dutch artist Joep van Lieshout. The sculpture route was set up during the pandemic as a getaway for the inhabitants of Rotterdam, to enjoy culture while being outside. Studio de Ronners was commissioned to develop the campaign with a website, posters, flyers, map and wayfinding. The concept was in the name: *Let's Get Physical*. The design played with the longing for physical contact, by placing the images of three iconic pieces by Joep Van Lieshout as big as possible, using tight margins, squished typography, *Arial Black* — a given design-requirement, and fleshy colours. In this way, the design creates rapprochement. Almost too close for comfort.

# UCR Arts

**Forth + Back / forthandback.la**
🌐 USA

UCR ARTS is an art museum and cultural center affiliated with the University of California Riverside. UCR ARTS is comprised of two connected institutions, The California Museum of Photography, and The Barbara and Art Culver Center of the Arts.

Forth + Back worked with the campus and the museum to create an entirely new graphic identity that was able to house these two art institutions (photography and contemporary art respectively) under one cohesive overhead brand.

# Crop

# IABR

Studio de Ronners / deronners.nl
⊕ The Netherlands

The International Architecture Biennial Rotterdam (IABR) deals with urgent questions about our environment such as climate change. Architects, designers and politicians are challenged to think about our future. For the eighth edition *Our Future in the Delta, the Delta of the Future*, Studio de Ronners came up with a clear and convincing way to communicate the IABR's serious, yet relevant themes by thinking radically and optimistically. They came up with 'Radical Optimism', with a radical visual language combined with optimistic colours. The campaign was translated in print, placed throughout Rotterdam, the exhibition design and an interactive installation.

Crop

# our future in the delta, the delta of the future

**international architecture biennale rotterdam**

### the miss

**NL**
De IABR heeft de editi
gezet van de Sustaina
Verenigde Naties en h

Hoe onvoorstelbaar o
blijven, dan zal hij zijn
inzicht vraagt om een
van alle dimensies va
Parijse Klimaatakkoor
klimaatverandering m
rijk rekenen: de bestri
inzetten op technolog
in infrastructuur zal he
opwarmen van de aar
omslag in onze interp
nodig. Zijn we hier col

Het eerste deel van h
'werkbiennale' met als
het ruimtelijk ontwerp
veroorzaakte klimaatv
om op te schalen en t
daadwerkelijk te hale

ierin ligt de essentië
dragsverandering n
weerbaar systeem op
sociale, ruimtelijke en
te koppelen, op de sc
planeet. In te ontwerp
herkenbaar zijn, die te
anlokkelijk en overtu

m die grote, veelom
nnen onderzoeken
rkgebied in eerste
helde Delta, de Del
men met vele partn
de delta en daarna,
toekomst weer ste
ze toekomst in de

## the missing link

EN
The IABR fully focuses its 2018 and 2020 editions on the Sustainable Development Goals (SDGs) of the United Nations and the Paris Climate Agreement.

No matter how hard it is to imagine: if we want our planet to remain livable for human beings, we will have to adapt our way of life. This insight calls for a fundamental pursuit of sustainability and it implies the adaptation of all dimensions of our lives. By signing the Paris Climate Agreement we subscribed to making mitigation of climate change a global priority. But we should not make the mistake of thinking that merely treating the symptoms will be enough. Depending on technological breakthroughs and massive infrastructural investments alone, we will not be able to preserve ecosystems and stop global warming, as this requires radically new interpretations of 'value,' 'prosperity,' and 'future.' Can we, collectively, pull this off?

The first half of the diptych IABR–2018+2020 is a 'work biennale' that centers on the following questions: How can spatial design effectively respond to human-made climate change? And what is keeping us from upscaling and accelerating so we can actually achieve the climate goals? What is THE MISSING LINK?

This is the essential design challenge we face: to facilitate the necessary behavioral changes and to upscale and accelerate the transition to a resilient system, we have to connect social, spatial and ecological issues at the level of the dwelling, the neighborhood, the city, and the entire planet. Designed alternatives have to communicate a new reality that is both realistic and concrete, both alluring and convincing. That is the task.

To investigate this huge task in a meaningful way, the IABR and the curators decided to look at the Rhine Meuse Scheldt Delta, the Delta of the Low Lands, first. Together with many partners, we will focus on our future in the Delta in 2018 and then, on the way to 2020, we will increasingly link the delta of the future to the world.
Our future in the Delta and the delta of the future.

Big Type

# Raquel Papers

**Marisa Piñana / marisapinana.com**
⊕ UK

Raquel Papers is a shop that sells books and school supplies in Benicarló, Spain.

Marisa Piñana was commissioned to promote the shop through low-cost advertising. The aim was to design three unique tote bags with a playful and distinctive visual language to catch the eye from a distance.

The composition uses words related to the shop (the name, street number, city and the year it was promoted) and plays with two shapes representing an open and closed book.

These tote bags are durable, reusable and therefore perfect for helping the environment.

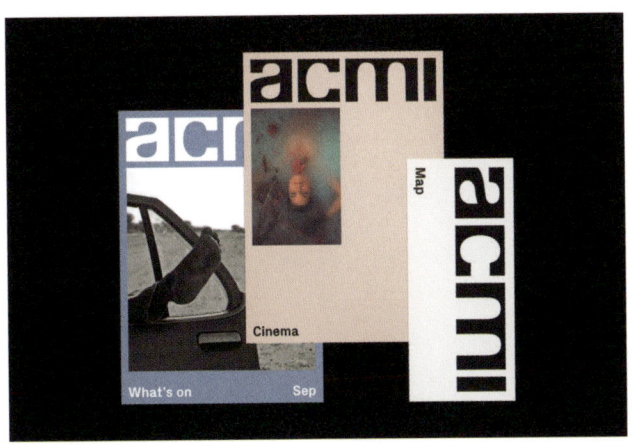

# ACMI

North / northdesign.co.uk
⊕ UK

By its nature, screen content is always moving and evolving and so must ACMI. In keeping with this, and the museum's progression to a fully integrated multiplatform experience, North designed a new overall system to be rolled out across the museum's physical assets and broad range of digital platforms. The bespoke new logo expresses the confidence of the renewed museum, standing alone as a central design element rather than a formality to be hidden in the bottom corner.

Crop

Big Type

# Phi Foundation for Contemporary Art – Yoko Ono

**Principal / principal.studio**
🌐 **Canada**

Given Yoko Ono's fame, it was not surprising that an exhibition covering the artist's 50-year career, so closely associated with performance and conceptual art, would arouse the general public's interest. The exhibition also coincided with a key moment for the institution, which was changing its name from DHC/ART to the Phi Foundation.

The communication's objective was therefore threefold: announce the presence of a major artist in the city; invite a new audience to visit the Phi Foundation; and communicate the name-change to loyal visitors. In collaboration with Phi, Principal's mandate was to produce a billboard campaign and to outline the main design interventions for the exhibition. Principal also designed both the website and the book that accompanied the exhibition throughout the world.

The exhibition signature interlaces the words 'Yoko' and 'Ono', thus rendering the intimate and participatory dimension of the artist's work. Used in the poster campaign and in communications, it quickly became iconic. An interactive version greeted users on entering the event's website.

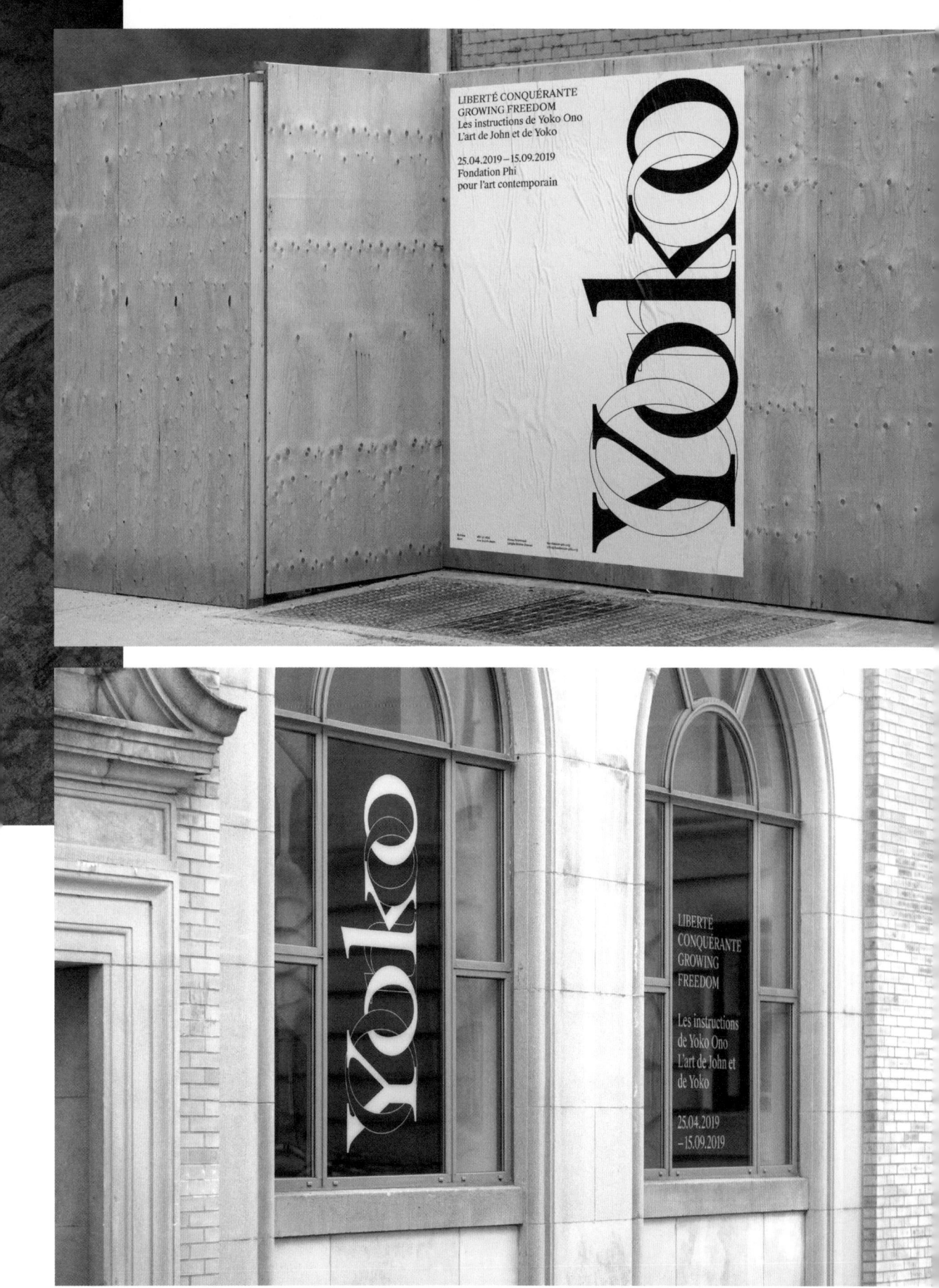

# CHAMP-DE-MARS

**LIBERTÉ CONQUÉRANTE**
**GROWING FREEDOM**

Les instructions de Yoko
L'art de John et de Yoko

Crop

# Independent Barcelona Coffee Festival 2018

Pràctica / practica.design
🌐 Spain

This 2018 campaign was created for the IBCF, Independent Barcelona Coffee Festival, an annual event that brings together professionals and fanatics of specialty coffee.

Photography: Bonastre.

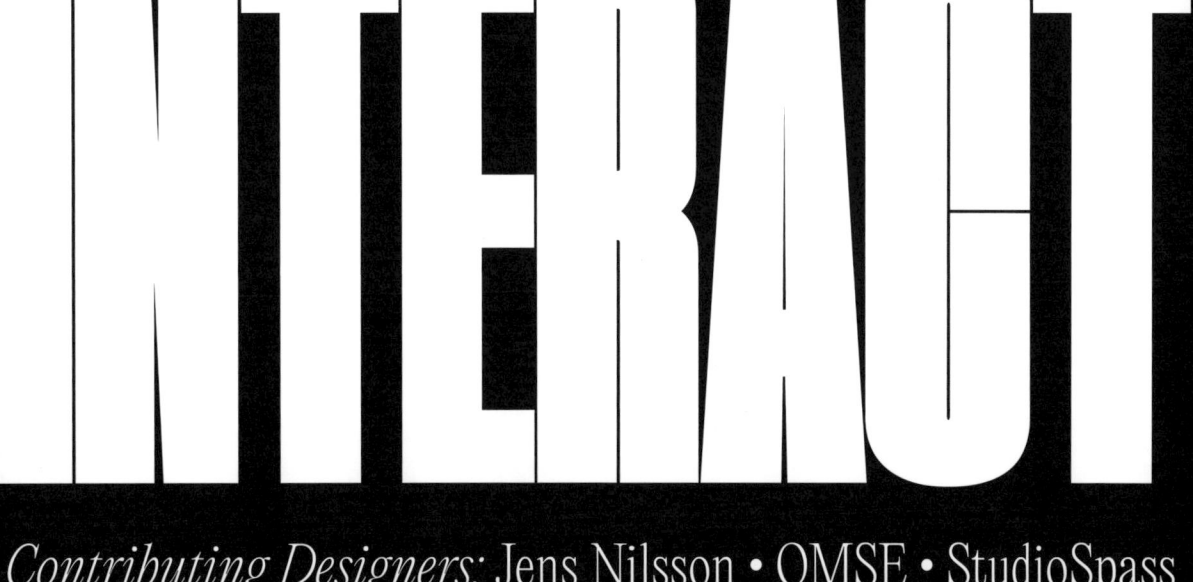

# INTERACT

*Contributing Designers:* Jens Nilsson • OMSE • StudioSpass
INTERVIEW • Domenic Lippa – Pentagram • León Romero →

# Malmöfestivalen

Jens Nilsson / jens-nilsson.com
🌐 Sweden

In 2014 Scandinavia's largest city festival celebrated 30 years of festivities. The grand party took place in August and roughly 1.4 million people visited the festival over eight consecutive days. To celebrate the festival's anniversary in style the largest physical graphic identity the world had ever seen was created: a gigantic physical art installation measuring 13×8 meters. The installation was interaction-friendly and visitors could jump, climb, or just plain chill on it.

2014's graphic identity for Malmöfestivalen has been featured in hundreds of articles around the world – *AdWeek*, *Creative Review*, *HOW Design* and many more. The praise from visitors in the streets and from the global creative community exceeded all expectations and the identity won a silver egg in the Swedish communication competition *Guldägget*.

# Printworks

OMSE / omse.co
🌐 UK

This augmented reality campaign was created by OMSE for Printworks London to promote its season of events. 3D typography was built upon the cultural venue's original identity by Only Studio, as well as its heritage as Europe's largest printing factory. The campaign appeared on giant billboards installed across London and other English cities, press advertisements, posters and online graphics. When viewed through the phone camera using a custom-built app, users were able to experience the 3D typographic animations come to life in immersive augmented reality, allowing them to move through the artwork, record photos or videos and share these online.

**Creative Agency:** OMSE & Family Type.
**Digital Studio:** Twomuch Studio.

Interact

Big Type

Interact

# So Me Thing Kunsthal

StudioSpass / studiospass.com
⊕ Netherlands

*So Me Thing* is an interactive installation created for the exhibition *Do it* at Kunsthal Rotterdam 2015. The piece, consisting of 50 layers of typography applied and divided over 7200 unique numbered pages, is StudioSpass' interpretation of Robert Barry's original *doit #93* (2012) for the exhibition manual by curator Hans Ullrich Orbist.

"Do something unique that only you and no one else in the world can do. Don't call it art."

The installation invites visitors to tear off sheets of paper to create their own typographic composition. By doing so, visitors playfully discover all the hidden typographic layers. The message 'So Me Thing' remains readable till the last layer is removed.

# INTERVIEW
## Studio Spass / Jaron Korvinus & Daan Mens

studiospass.com
🌐 Netherlands

Atelier Wartaal. Photography: Aad Hoogendoorn.

Studio Spass is a Rotterdam-based agency that works across print, branding, web and spatial design projects as well as animation and photography. Founded by Jaron Korvinus and Daan Mens in 2008, the studio combines a rigorous, considered and intelligent approach with a playful sensibility.

Typojanchi International Typography Biennale Seoul. Photography: Kim Jinsol.

### What is your background and how did you become involved in graphic design?

Daan and I both actually started studying illustration at the Willem de Kooning Academy in Rotterdam. We were never in the same study year but nevertheless we became friends during a school trip to New York for the whole illustration department. During our studies we were spending most of our time sketching and experimenting at the printmaking facilities. We got more interested in graphic design because, besides making nice images, we also wanted to design and decide how the whole publication, product or project would look like. This led to following the courses at the graphic design department, internships at agencies and eventually graduating as a more complete designer and starting the studio.

### How would you describe your creative style and process?

Our design approach always starts with gathering information, making jokes and creating several sketches and concepts. Every new project, commission or collaboration has a unique context. This context always gives us a lot of inspiration in the concept phase. One of the nicest things about being a designer is that you have the chance to become a temporary specialist on all kinds of different subjects. We also spend a lot of time debating and talking about our sketches. This seems to be our way of fixing loose ends in the concept and preparing for a presentation. Nine out of ten times we prefer to present just a single concept. For us it feels more convincing when we truly believe in a concept.

### Typography has a strong prominence in your portfolio. Why is type so important to your work?

Type is an amazing and fun system to make language and communicate. We use language in our work as a tool to create interaction. We like to convert language within our projects into surprising new forms. Playing and experimenting with language and type design is something we really love working on.

### How would you define good typography?

Typography is good when it communicates and creates interaction. This can be functional; for example when it makes you read a text, triggers you to go to an event or enter a store. But also decorative typefaces can provoke an action or emotion.

**Do you have a favourite font and why?**

Yes, we have the *Favorit* font by Dinamo. We like design and typefaces that somehow stand the test of time and taste. That's always easier to judge when looking back at your projects after a while.

**What are your main goals and considerations when working on spatial design?**

We love to sketch in 3D with simple paper studies or cardboard models. This fun and analogue way of working leaves more space open for coincidence in a sketch process. Walking around and spending time with these experiments and models make it easier for us to spot the designs with the most potential. Our approach to spatial design is about making an impact or connection first. We design for people, so an object or mural should be there and make an impression and hopefully drag you out of your daily routine. Functionality and usability are also important in making that impression last in a good way. We really want our designs to be used by people. The materialisation is also very important. Through time we've learned that the most sustainable way of making spatial design is by using high quality and long lasting materials.

**In terms of scale, what are the challenges of spatial design compared to screen or print?**

When we execute a project size, weight and logistics are always important. For example, sometimes something really big needs to be built in separate parts because it needs to fit through a small entry door. The bigger a project the bigger the team and the more you have to rely on the skills of the professionals that are executing your idea. Knowing what we can't do was part of our learning curve, in time we really had to surround our studio with people that have other specialisms.

**What do you think of the design scene in Rotterdam today? How has it evolved?**

Rotterdam is a real harbour city that was heavily damaged during the second world war. It got rebuilt with loads of urban planning and architectural experiments and therefore the city has quite a unique DNA within the Netherlands. This is also what attracted us to study there in the first place. When we graduated in 2008 it wasn't the most obvious route to directly start a studio. In my memory, we were one of the only ones to begin in Rotterdam that year.

For creatives Rotterdam was a great place to live and work. The city was quite unpopular, had almost no tourism, many vacant buildings and therefore low rents. There was a lively bottom-up artistic scene and a good design ecosystem. It was a great city to start a studio in and it offered us a lot of possibilities. Rotterdam was and is of course mostly known for its famous architecture firms.

Nowadays there is a very high density of artists, architects and designers but a lot of the output they create is more for the national and global market. Over the last years more studios and initiatives have found their way into Rotterdam. It also became much more of a goal for young, freshly graduated designers to start their own independent studios. The majority of us are relaxed and have an open mentality, so I guess this only leads to more collaborations, exchange of knowledge and projects. Maybe even a bit of positive competition as well. As in every city gentrification and investment capitalism has made its entry in the last couple of years and is changing and threatening the whole way of how the city functions.

**You were founded in 2008. After over ten years in the industry, how has your design studio evolved?**

Since the start we aimed to keep the core of the studio small while making the projects, clients and ambitions grow. Keeping it small made our studio fun and flexible. As our studio name might suggest, this fun is really a core part of our studio's DNA (in German 'Spass' means fun). We try to have fun in the design process, and this should somehow translate or communicate to the end result and its users. In terms of flexibility it means we can cherry pick those collaborations and projects we love working on. It feels good not to have money as the leading incentive for projects.

In the early years our studio was organising a lot of exhibitions and initiated several collaborations. Then for a couple of years we focussed more on including those efforts into commissioned projects. Now that we've figured that out, over the last few years we also find a lot of joy in making free work and publishing collaborative experiments again. This also led to the start of our own Spass shop.

Kunstblock
↓ ZigZagCity

Interact

Big Type

# Atelier Wartaal

**StudioSpass** / studiospass.com
🌐 Netherlands

*Wartaal* is a playground for language and performing arts StudioSpass has designed at contemporary art gallery TENT Rotterdam. *Wartaal* is a collaborative project by TENT Rotterdam, Theater Rotterdam, writer Raoul de Jong and StudioSpass. Visitors are invited to make their first steps in this magical world and discover what performance art is and does. In addition to performance as an art form, language is also an important theme. A full alphabet of 26 activities makes visitors perform and explore language in various ways.

The playful typography system the studio designed plays the main visual role and can be found everywhere within the space. All interactive elements have been designed in a red colour to make visitors navigate the space intuitively. It encourages visitors to play, make and discover terrain in which they are challenged to shape their view of the world. To get visitors in the right head space an introductory video was made that also serves as the secret entrance into the space. In the video, visitors are encouraged to dress up, compile their own 'letter suit' and jump into the adventure. The biomorph visual language of Dada artist Hans Arp served as inspiration for the original floor plan design.

Dadaism is a great inspiration overall for *Wartaal;* Dada artists radically returned to their childish creativity and let chance play a major role in the creation of their work. In poetry, the Dadaists wrote absurd poems full of incoherent nonsense, sometimes consisting only of pure sounds. Collage and assembly were commonly used techniques. In addition, Dada artists often created temporary art such as performances. It was originally a very politically committed, pacifist movement of left-thinking artists who opposed society. This resistance, or at least making your voice heard, whether or not in the form of protest, has a place in the project.

**Photography:** Aad Hoogendoorn.

# LDF 2020

Big Type

Domenic Lippa – Pentagram / pentagram.com
🌐 UK

In 2020 LDF's Design Director Domenic Lippa designed the Festival's identity for the 14th consecutive year, creating posters, wayfinding and signage, merchandise, digital content and advertising as well as the printed Festival guide. The aim was to develop a campaign that would be instantly recognisable, and would reinforce the vital role of the creative industries during what was a challenging year. As with previous identities, the signature colour palette of red and white was employed – this is now one of the Festival's strongest and most recognisable assets. The identity uses a series of expanded letterforms which grow to fill the space available, making us consider our own spaces and the different ways we now have to fit into them.

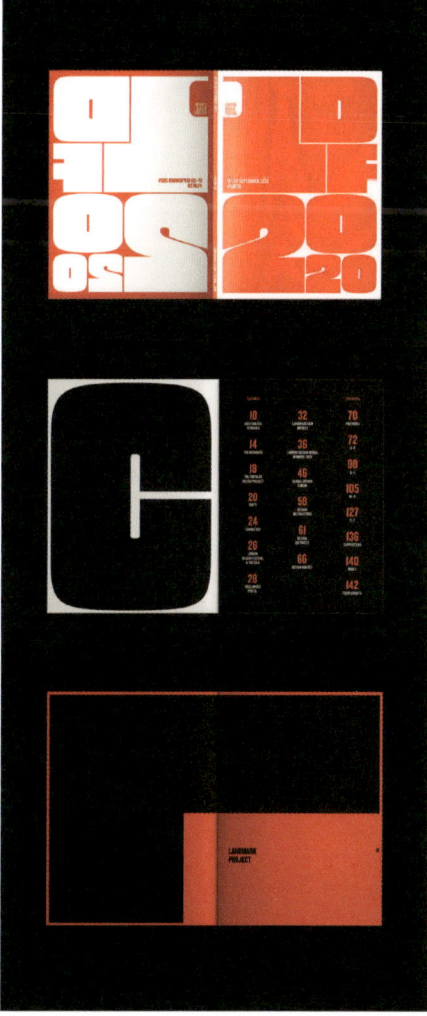

Interact

# Eh! Tallers d'Estiu per Joves

León Romero / leonromero.work
🌐 Spain

Campaign development for the project *Eh! Tallers d'Estiu per Joves* (Summer Workshops for Youth), a proposal that stems from CCCB during confinement, with the idea to provide opportunities in the neighbourhood and get adolescents closer to culture through workshops related to music, dance, serigraphy and audiovisuals.

Since the main audience are between the age of 14 and 18, it seeks to impact through new ways of communication, with content creation for different social networks and a supporting campaign of printed pieces, which were placed in strategic spots to captivate the main target audience's attention.

With the circumstances of this commission, the social context and the audience, the outcome is a digital native campaign; simple but very expressive, in which the very same digital language resources, such as the oral writing, animation, stickers or gifs from the social networks are appropriated to create rich, urban and dynamic compositions.

The result is a spectrum of layouts with different artworks in the shape of the word 'Eh!' which works as an element to captivate people's attention in both a casual and immediate way. It engages with the visual language of the target audience in a one-on-one conversation, inviting them to interact with the applications and campaign pieces, which call for them to become participants in the workshops.

dilluns—divendres 17:30-20h
inscripció prèvia
www.cccb.org

# tallers per a joves 06.07— 10.09.20 CCCB

art urbà pinay, arts marcials, audiovisual, autorepresentació i *selfies*, dansa contemporània, danses urbanes, dibuix amb codi, fanzines, ràdio i podcasting, rap i hip hop, serigrafia

# talleres jóvenes 06.07— 10.09.20 CCCB

arte urbano pinay
artes marciales
audiovisual
autorrepresentación
danza contemporá
danzas urbanas
dibujo con código
fanzines
radio y podcasting
rap y hip hop
serigrafía

art urbà pinay
arts marcials
audiovisual
autorepresentació i *selfies*
dansa contemporània
danses urbanes
dibuix amb codi
fanzines
ràdio i podcasting
rap i hip hop
serigrafia

dilluns—divendres
17:30-20h
inscripció prèvia
www.cccb.org

tallers per a joves 06.07—10.09.20 CCCB

lunes—viernes
17:30-20h
inscripción previa
www.cccb.org

# CONDENSED

*Contributing Designers:* My Name is Wendy Studio
• Lukas Diemling • Twoo • F61 Agency • Forth + Back
• Max Friedman • Jack Forrest INTERVIEW • Jens Nilsson
• Studio de Ronners →

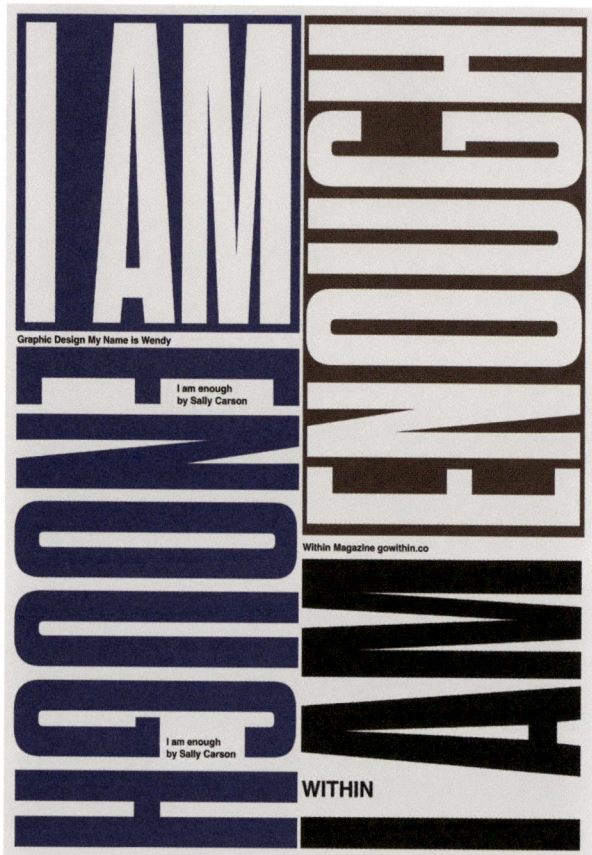
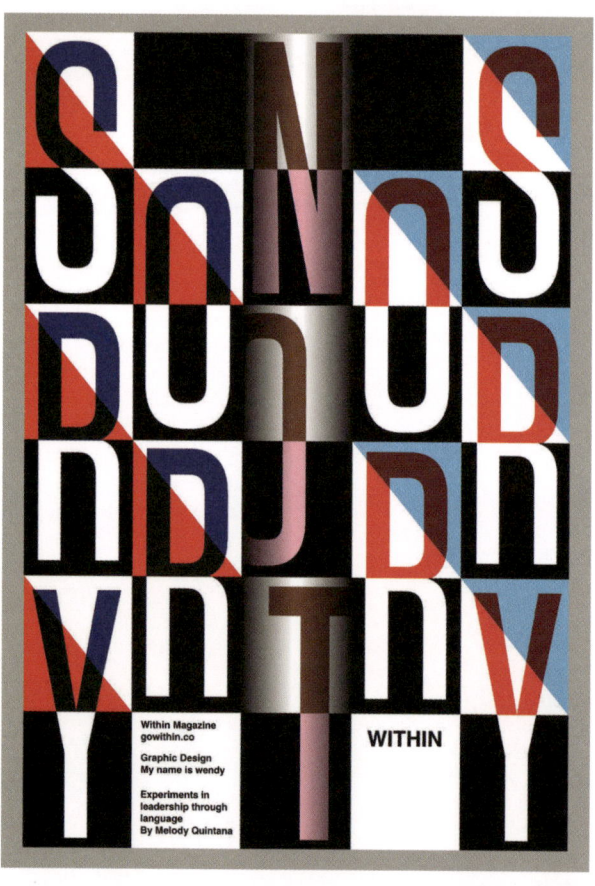

# Within Magazine

**My Name is Wendy Studio / mynameiswendy.fr**
⊕ France

*Within Magazine* exists to do three things: challenge the status quo of leadership in design and technology, share practical wisdom for creating environments where all people thrive and amplify stories of more diverse leaders.

More than a magazine, *Within* is a community that is driving design towards a more diverse and inclusive future.

Within Magazine
gowithin.co

Graphic Design
My name is wendy

I am enough
By Sally Carson

WITHIN

I AM ENOUGH ENOUGH

Condensed

Big Type

# FIMI

### Lukas Diemling / diemling.com
⊕ Austria

Lukas Diemling created a brand identity that perfectly matches the characteristics of this mechatronics and locksmith practice from Austria: simple and strong, bold and timeless, but with just the right amount of emotion and zeitgeist. The custom wordmark which is the short version of the name *Fink Michael* is used very large, edge to edge, on all materials.

Condensed

# Galeria Index

Twoo / wearetwoo.com
🌐 USA

Both garish and graceful, the Galeria Index identity combines a distinctly digital green colour with an essentially Brazilian typography; both representing the solidity of Brazil and the modernity of its new artists.

*Vinila* typeface is characterised by the ink-traps found across its diverse range of weights, and its bolder styles for commanding headlines, or its elegant lighter weights for body copy and supporting information.

For the gallery's new online presence, the solution was intended to convey the feeling of an index by using organised layouts capable of holding dense amounts of information.

Finding inspiration in yellow list-style books of old, the index concept appears offline as well, with an A to Z style list of employed artists to represent the zeitgeist of the local art scene across printed ephemera and merchandise.

Condensed

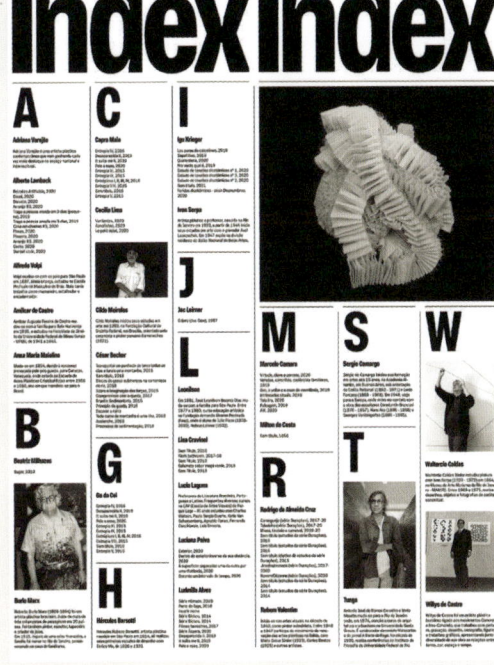

Condensed

Big Type

# Habit

**F61 Agency / f61agency.com**
🌐 Russia

Habit is a bright and ambitious project created by professionals with extensive experience in the coffee industry. One of the main aspirations of Habit is to create a habit of living freely and brightly in a world where each cup of coffee is not just a drink prepared by the skillful hands of a barista, but also an emotion that sets the tone for the whole day.

The name 'Habit' and the brand's philosophy became the starting point for F61 Agency to develop the visual identity. Habit is a project about more than coffee, it is about emotions, freedom and the habit of treating yourself.

Bright and bold, it tells us: "A bad day? – Maybe coffee?", "A good day? – Coffee?" No matter what happens and wherever you are – find the time to treat yourself.

F61 Agency tried to reflect all these ideas in the branding, where the logo is a dynamic, free form that can fill the entire surface, hide in a corner, or even start dancing around with the slogan – the features of complete freedom.

**Photography:** Lana Lomakina / Daniil Zherdev.

Big Type

Cold brew coffee

**250**

Habit

**COLD BREW COFFEE**

COCOA & VANILLA

Region: Guji / Roast: espresso / Processing method: Natu
Arabica variety: Mixed heirloom
Taste: sweet balanced coffee with notes of blackberry,
red orange and dark grape

# SPIRAL

## TRIBALISM
ISSUE I

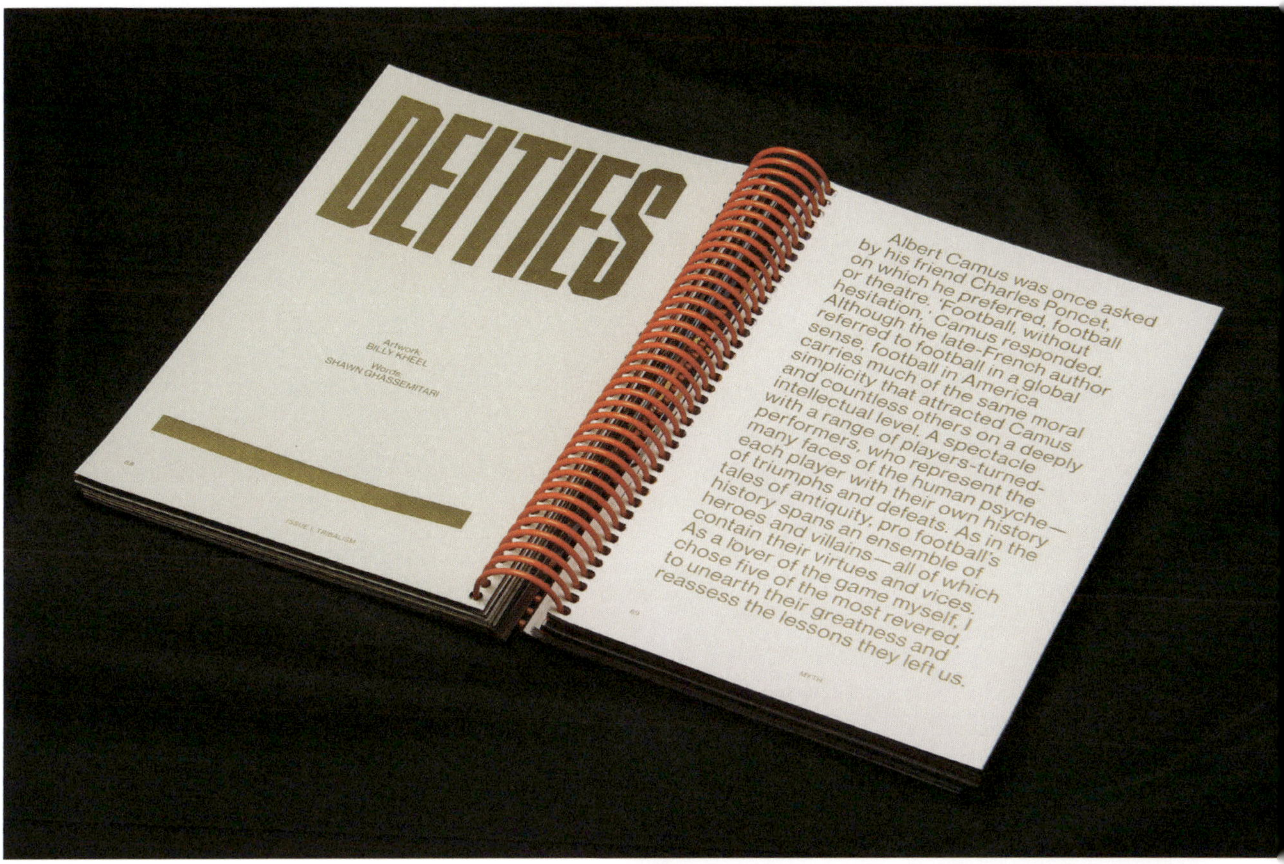

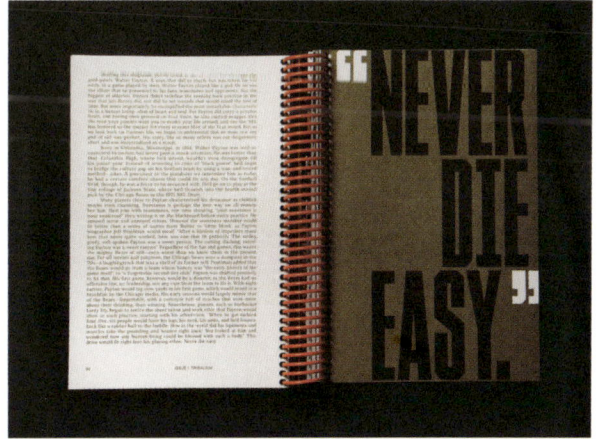

# Spiral Journal

Forth + Back / forthandback.la
⊕ USA

*Spiral* is a print publication that bridges the gap between football and culture. Printed annually, each issue explores a theme that connects the culture surrounding the game through the worlds of sport, art, design, music and fashion.

The first issue aimed to both celebrate and challenge the diverse world of football by highlighting the game's storied yet troublesome history, observing the many relics and traditions shared by fans, discussing the players and 'superfans' who have rose to mythic proportions, along with speaking to an array of creatives, athletes, and individuals who are all pushing football forward.

153

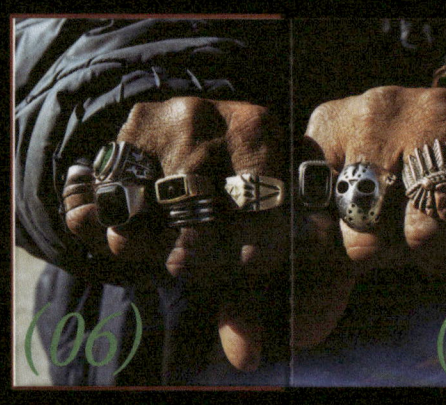

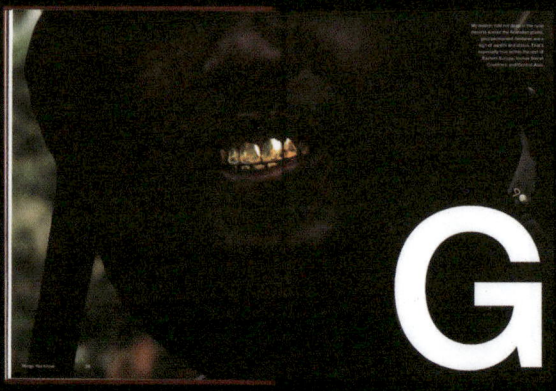

154

## Things You Know

Max Friedman / maxbfriedman.com
⊕ USA

Filmmaker Jamil McGinnis and Max Friedman documented the mile-wide neighbourhood of Crown Heights in Brooklyn, New York for two years.

Friedman's publication *Things You Know* is a 260-page collection of photographs, writings and found objects from that time exploring concepts of home, dissimilation and coexistence. 100% of profits from the project went towards creating a photography program with the Launch Charter School in Crown Heights in the summer of 2021, which culminated in a gallery exhibition at the Weeksville Heritage Museum.

Big Type

# NICE!

Max Friedman / maxbfriedman.com
🌐 USA

Photographed over the course of six months between New York and New Jersey, *NICE!* is a 210-page visual journal that attempts to capture the surreally self-reflective spirit of 2020.

# INTERVIEW
## Jack Forrest

cheersjack.com
🌐 Australia

Daily Poster Project

Jack Forrest is a multidisciplinary designer based in Sydney. He actively utilises all forms of design and technology to create work with depth and impact. Jack believes in the power of design to influence opinion, shift behaviours and make people happy.

↑ Forbes Spain
Love at First Sight

**What is your background and how did you become involved in graphic design?**

I got into design by watching a heap of different YouTube, Photoshop and Illustrator tutorials. YouTube has thousands (if not millions) of well-made, comprehensive tutorials from amazing creators that are free to watch.

It was by watching and following these tutorials that I slowly gained an introduction into the Adobe Creative Suite and the infinite potential for creating anything and everything. Once I had a handle on how to use the more fundamental features of these programs, I loved (and still love) spending time experimenting with the different niche tools and functions to just see what happened and if it looked fun or interesting. This lead to me studying a Bachelor of Design in Visual Communication course at the University of Technology Sydney.

**How would you describe your creative style and process?**

I wouldn't say I have a strict process, but instead that I rely on experimentation. I like to spend as much time as possible on the tools, playing around with different images, graphics and type until I find compositions that feel balanced.

By taking this approach, I'm accepting that design isn't a linear process and I am embracing all the uncertainty that comes with it and (hopefully) finding outcomes that are unique and engaging.

**Typography has a strong prominence in your portfolio. Why is type so important to your work?**
I think it adds another level to the work and makes it more interesting. The type acts as a way for me to inform the other elements on the page. For example, in the posters with bigger, bolder type it can add dimensionality to the images used. I also just like big letters. We're so used to seeing characters at a certain, small, scale that we rarely appreciate the craft in the construction of each letter. When you blow type up to this larger size, you're looking at something which is both familiar but also unknown.

**How would you define good typography?**
Typography is good when it integrates seamlessly with other elements in the design. Whether the type is included as a minor supporting element or as a strong centre piece, it should work with surrounding elements to create a piece that is greater than the sum of its parts.

**Do you have a favourite font and why?**
Probably *Woodland* by Pangram Pangram Foundry. It's a unique, personality-packed, curvy serif with a lovely weight variation throughout. I've found that *Woodland* pairs quite nicely with my illustration style as the thinner moments in the characters match the stroke weight of the illustrations. In these illustrative posters, I love that the type can add a distinct personality that wouldn't be otherwise achievable.

**In your spare time, you challenge yourself to design (almost) daily posters. Can you tell us how this project came about?**
I started this project in early March 2020 as COVID-19 saw me spending more and more time sitting around at home. At the same time, I was going into my final year of university and I was looking for ways to improve my portfolio and start creating a point of difference for myself as I began searching for my first full-time design gig.

**What are your main goals and considerations when working on personal projects such as this?**
Ultimately, I'm just looking for ways to grow and improve as a designer. I wanted to try and make something (almost) every single day and fingers crossed after a couple months, these things would look better than they did when I started.

**What drives you creatively?**
I'm largely driven by the amazing work of other designs that I see on platforms like Instagram. I've found that by immersing myself in this global creative community, I'm consistently exposed to individuals from all over the world creating unique, beautiful content. The rich variety of this work reminds me of the infinite possibilities when designing and drives me to continue experimenting with each piece of content.

Roomies

I've found that by immersing myself in this global creative community, I'm consistently exposed to individuals from all over the world creating unique, beautiful content. The rich variety of this work reminds me of the infinite possibilities when designing and drives me to continue experimenting with each piece of content.

# Daily Poster Series

Jack Forrest / cheersjack.com
🌐 Australia

In his spare time, Jack Forrest challenges himself to design (almost) daily posters exploring a variety of subject matters and experimenting with different graphic styles. It's through these posters that he can test type and colour combinations, as well as experimental layouts of text and image, to then be deployed across other design applications. These posters are shared via his Instagram feed @cheersjack.

Condensed

# Forest Gum

**Jens Nilsson / jens-nilsson.com**
🌐 Sweden

Forest Gum is a German natural chewing gum that is made from tree sap, and not plastic like pretty much every other gum is made of.

During 2019 Jens Nilsson worked on this identity and packaging design together with Thomas and Maren from Forest Gum. The first flavour is now available in selected stores in Germany.

Condensed

# Print is Not Dead

**Studio de Ronners / deronners.nl**
🌐 The Netherlands

Is print dead? Not in the opinion of Studio de Ronners. As a design agency, they believe in the importance of print, while embracing the digital world at the same time. In a triptych of 'paper animations', they played with the idea of analog versus digital by translating the aesthetics of paper to a digital medium.

The motion graphics visualise paper being torn, each new layer revealing a statement related to paper: "Let's Wrap This Up", "Let's Tear It Down", "Let's Keep On Rollin'". Their animated poster series was selected for the DEMO (Design in Motion) Festival, that took place in November 2019. During the Festival, all selected motion designs by the best designers and studios were shown on digital screens at Amsterdam Central Station.

# STRETCH

*Contributing Designers:* Marina Willer – Pentagram • Hingston Studio • PORTO ROCHA • Campbell Hay INTERVIEW • HelloMe • A Black Cover Design (ABCD) • León Romero • Only →

Stretch

# Moholy-Nagy Foundation

Marina Willer – Pentagram / pentagram.com
🌐 UK

The Moholy-Nagy Foundation asked Marina Willer to create a new identity and website to promote, research and preserve the legacy of László Moholy-Nagy's life and work. The mindset and methods used by Moholy-Nagy directly informed the craft-based approach. Unique typographic forms were created by hand in the studio using projections with light and water – these intriguing letterforms form the basis of the fluid identity and the distinctive typographic wordmark. Using techniques inspired by the artist's experimental approach, Marina Willer and her team created a striking and sympathetic identity that perfectly honours Moholy-Nagy's amazing legacy.

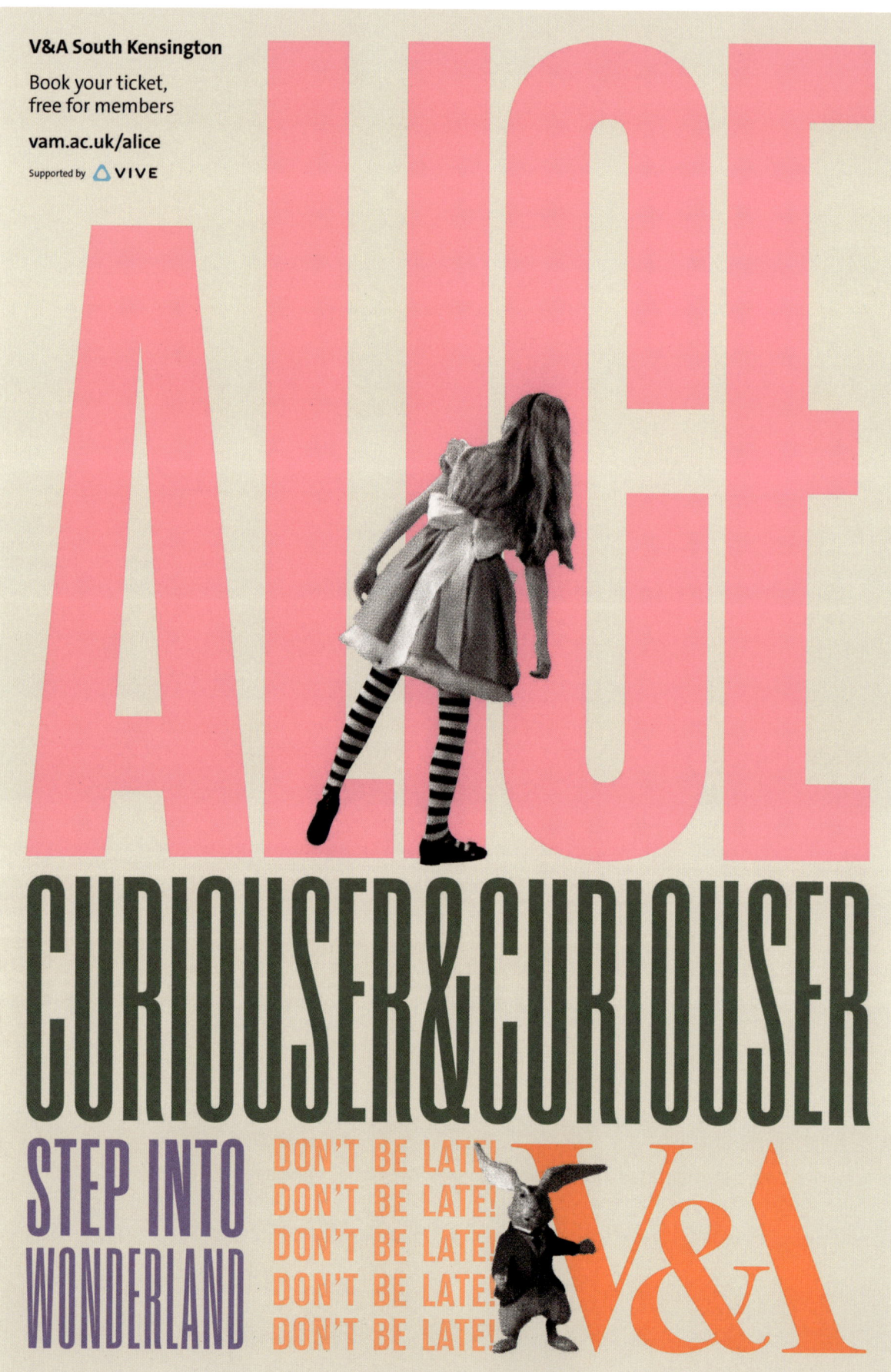

# Alice: Curiouser & Curiouser

Big Type

Hingston Studio / hingston.net
🌐 UK

This exhibition examined the transcendence of Alice, throughout the last 150 years across fashion, film, theatre, music, literature and art. With a multi-layered story to tell, the campaign employed a bold typographic approach, acting as a playful framework to host a mix of messaging, which would be evolved and embellished over the duration of the show. A contemporary take on the vernacular of vintage Circus posters, the campaign messaging plays with a repeated call to action as its lead voice, "Step Into Wonderland!", "See the Amazing…", "Don't be Late!".

In a nod to the story's famed exploration of perspective and size, the responsive typographic system is elastic in behaviour, allowing the campaign to perform in a dynamic way in digital environments. Letterforms themselves have an inherent stretch, flex and elasticity — shrinking, squeezing and expanding into any given space — or indeed, format.

**Design and Art Direction:** Hingston Studio.
**Puppet Makers:** Jonny & Will.
**3D Modelling and Animation:** Hingston Studio.
**Live Action Producer:** Rob Jelley.
**DoP:** Clouded Vision.
**Styling:** Arabella Boyce.

# Comrade

### PORTO ROCHA / portorocha.com
### 🌐 USA

In her political essay *Comrade* (Verso, 2019), Jodi Dean asserts that, "to be a comrade is to announce a belonging." This thesis informed the assertive, brutalist approach to the cover design, in which 'comrade' occupies every printable inch. The pronounced, blocky typography draws inspiration from Russian Constructivism, a movement instrumental in shaping the graphic style associated with the political comrade. The cover's visceral design creates a lasting impact by using a communication strategy reminiscent of earlier propaganda, fusing old and new. Unapologetic, all-red typography against a stark white stock announces the arrival of a camaraderie for our contemporary political moment.

# INTERVIEW
## Campbell Hay / Charlie Hay

campbellhay.com
🌐 UK

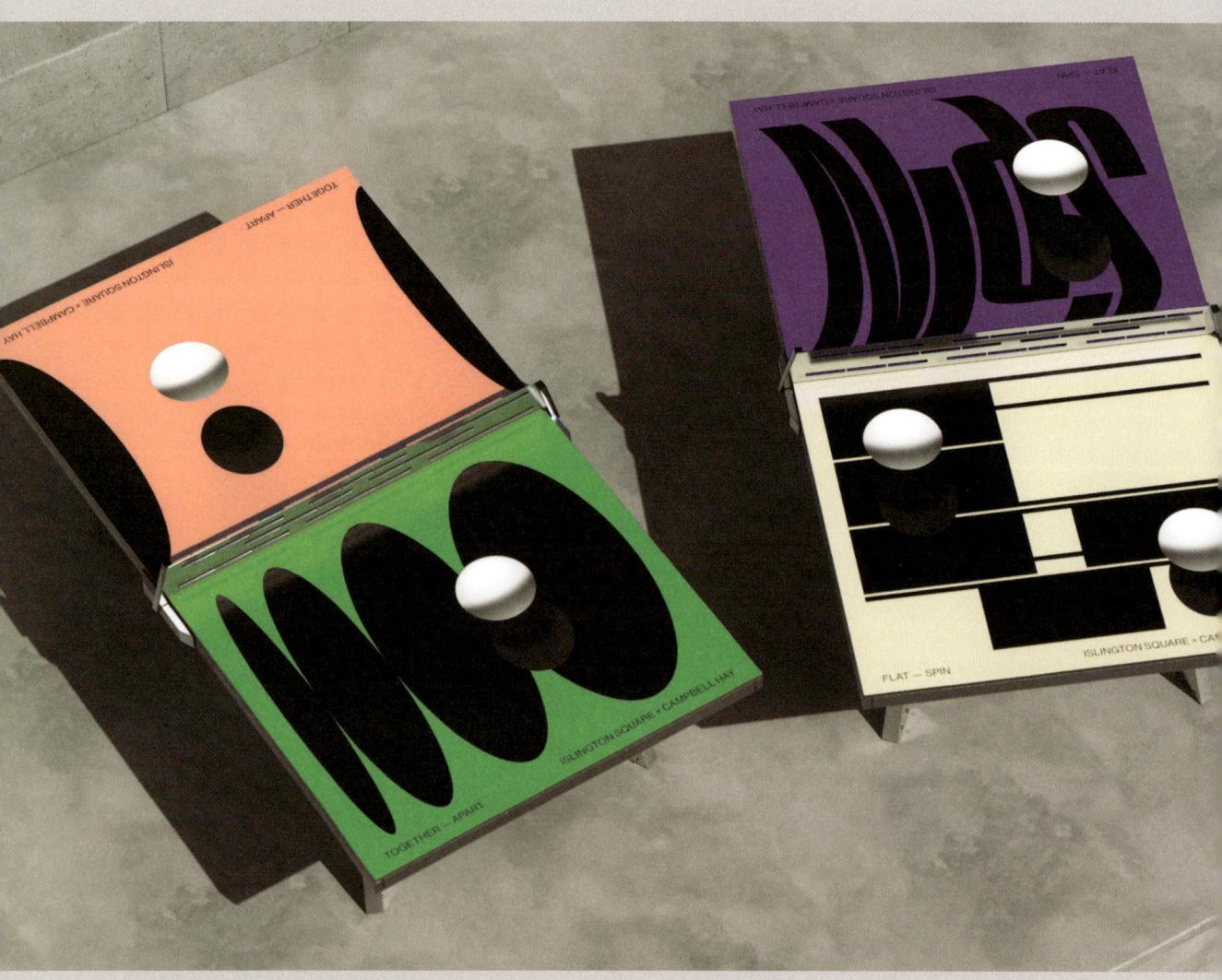

Art Tables for The Art of Ping Pong

Campbell Hay are a brand consultancy who believe that intelligent and beautiful design has the ability to create better and more joyful experiences for their customers. Working in partnership with their clients they uncover insights, define propositions and develop narratives that are brought to life with precision and imagination. The result — emotionally engaging brands built on clear ideas.

IQL

**What is your background and how did you become involved in graphic design?**
I studied at Saint Martins and spent a lot of time with friends in the various faculties around the college. I was studying Product Design but I loved the Graphics department; learning about print processes and typography.

After graduation I began working for a design agency that worked with large brands and I was able to be involved with all the specialisms at that point. I relished being part of the overarching brand process. I've never looked back.

**How would you describe your creative style and process?**
As a studio we take a reductive approach to design. Where possible we try to remove noise so the concept is clear and intelligible. Having said this, we try not to have a 'house style'. Instead we develop concepts through a research-based explorative process that celebrates the unique qualities of each project. We're always looking forward and searching for new ways to combine ideas and technologies.

**Typography has a strong prominence in your portfolio. Why is type so important to your work?**
Typography has such a powerful ability to set the tone within a brand or design project. It's like a person's voice; powerful or discreet, quirky or serious. The typography adds expression and personality.

The letterforms themselves are also really beautiful. You can play around with them, making them the subject of the design and creating something unexpected.

Above all else, it's an important consideration within the design process. When you're trying to make a point, you choose your words carefully. It's the same with typography, you just need the right font.

# Stretch

Le Grand Bazar
→ The Art Studio

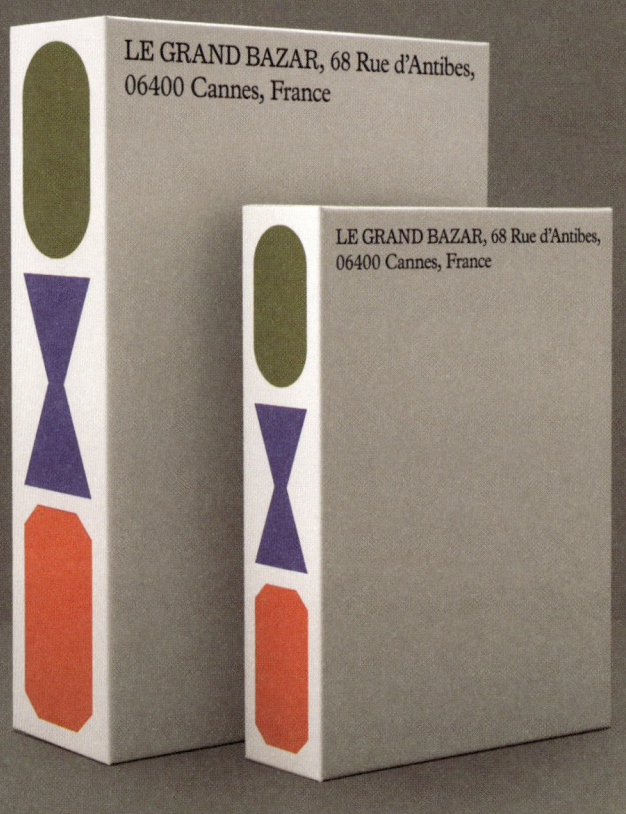

### How would you define good typography?
Good typography can be classified in one of two ways; expressive or functional. Both are well crafted, but in different ways.

Expressive typography should be emotive, bold and clearly articulate its purpose. It's noticeable and memorable. It articulates the tone of the communication.

Then there is functional typography. It's considered and balanced. Quieter; it doesn't want to be the centre of attention. It can take ages to get just right.

### Do you have a favourite font and why?
I remember in the early 00s Experimental Jetset created all their work using Helvetica. Sometimes I wish we could do the same — it would certainly save a lot of time. But we just don't love it that much. It's really hard to pick just one typeface because of our approach and the way each project is researched. We try and select a typeface that's fit for purpose and also satisfies our search for new ideas. We love working with some of the new typefaces release by some of the brilliantly talented foundries.

### How can effective design enhance a brand's identity?
Well researched and executed design nearly always enhances a brand's identity. Well researched and crafted design that draws on the team's experience and imagination is going to be more emotionally engaging, articulates the brand's values more clearly and keeps it relevant.

### In a world in which we are spending time online, being bombarded by messaging, is there a greater need for simpler, more direct identity design?
I think there's always been a need for simpler, more direct identity design. The temptation to add another promotional message or call to action has always been there, but it is perhaps more obvious now.

Design is so often consumed digitally today which opens a new set of opportunities for designers. The temptation to add motion and interaction is always there. Ultimately it's great to add a new dimension to a brand's identity, but it needs to be carefully considered and enhance the overall brand delivery, not distract it.

### What do you think of the design scene in London today? How has it evolved?
I think the London scene still manages to thrive despite all the challenges designers in the city face today.

It's been really interesting over the last decade. As the internet has accelerated the dissemination of ideas, trends have spread around the world with increasing pace. Platforms like Behance and Instagram create these mass aesthetic shifts that very quickly run their course.

So where do new ideas emerge? I think real-world places like London that celebrate diversity and bring together lots of inspirational ideas in one place.

The scene today still attracts design talent from around the world and design is ultimately a collaborative endeavour that benefits from that diversity.

**What drives you creatively?**
I think designers are generally optimistic and I think that drives you on creatively. And we're also a bit impatient, so eager to explore what's next.

Design is so often consumed digitally today which opens a new set of opportunities for designers. The temptation to add motion and interaction is always there. Ultimately it's great to add a new dimension to a brand's identity, but it needs to be carefully considered and enhance the overall brand delivery, not distract it.

# Art Tables

Campbell Hay / campbellhay.com
🌐 UK

Campbell Hay collaborated with The Art of Ping Pong to create eight uniquely designed ping pong tables. Inspired by the theme of opposing states, the graphics designed by Campbell Hay capture the dynamic nature and signature moves of ping pong.

With the use of Instagram filters, the typographic tables are further brought to life through animation and augmented reality. Through vibrant colours, bold and animated typography, the designs express the joy of the game — watch the tables bounce, smash and block.

# Nike, NBA All-Star 2020

**HelloMe / hellome.studio**
⊕ Germany

HelloMe developed the visual identity and branding for Nike's presence at *NBA All-Star 2020* — the biggest basketball event of the year.

Inspired by the unique characteristics of the 2020 host city Chicago, the hyper-vibrant colour system translates the city's transportation map into a contemporary palette, reflecting the diversity of the local communities while amplifying the city's buzzing youth culture. The custom slab-serif typeface *HM Chicago* forms the central component of the identity, equally drawing influence from the city's historic type specimens, and its iconic sports logos. Paired with *Futura*, *HM Chicago* forms part of a larger type system reflecting Nike's inseparable connection to Chicago's basketball history.

Stretch

# EDITOR

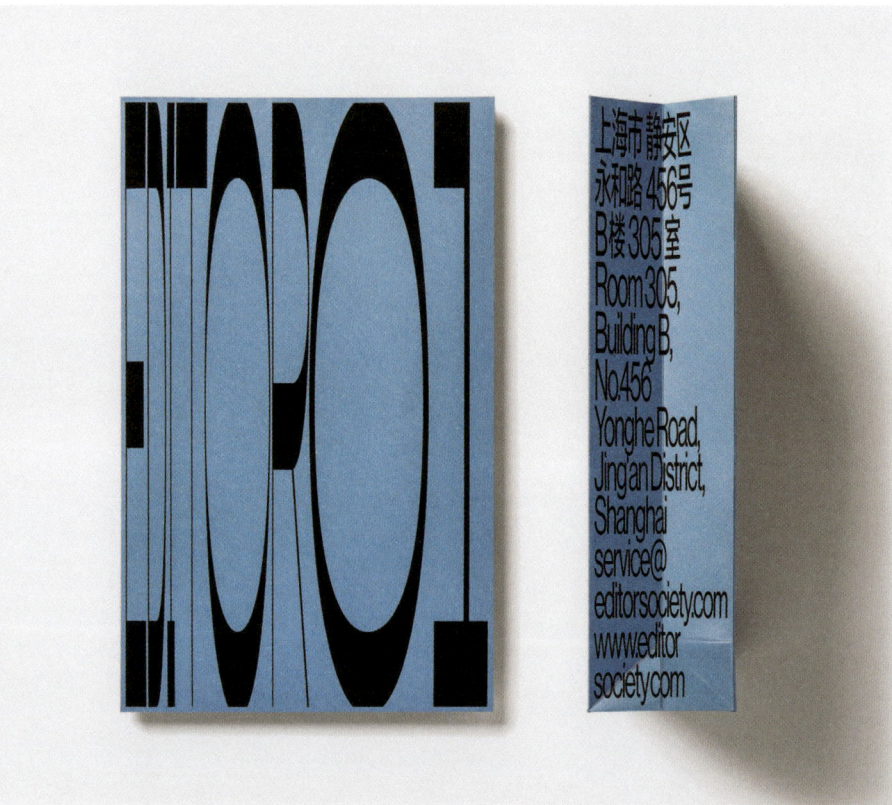

A Black Cover Design (ABCD) / ablackcover.com
🌐 China / USA

EDITOR is a brand new integrated business mode and has extremely high requirements for the expansive nature and uniqueness of design language.

After several rounds of discussion, ABCD decided to find a design language that, 'almost no one had done before', for EDITOR which is prospective, easy-to-operate and expandable.

The design is conceived with the literal meaning of 'EDITOR' as a starting point. Using an editor's thinking pattern: an image is defined as a content space to be filled with information. This is an operation mode that copes with changes by sticking to a fundamental principle. *EDITOR VI System* can be used to produce different design layouts to meet different content requirements and is highly identifiable.

In the design of EDITOR, building a visual system is more important than designing a beautiful layout. More precisely, ABCD have designed an information processing method not an image. This is why EDITOR has its own unique aesthetic taste.

Stretch

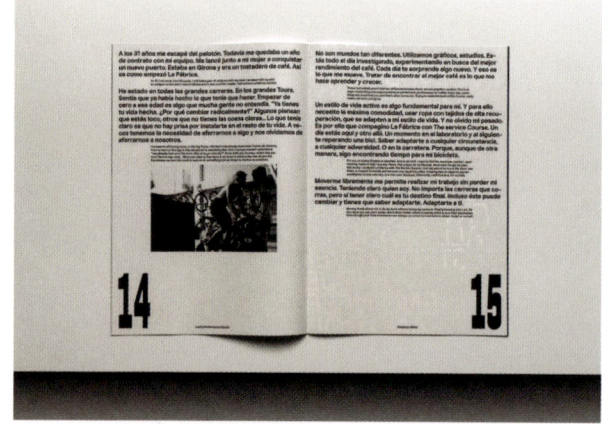

# Levi's

Big Type

León Romero / leonromero.work
 Spain

From the idea to portray different profiles of talented people who turn their work into a lifestyle, the creative agency Helsinki, in close collaboration with Studio Bruma, commissioned León Romero to conceptualise and design a publication as a supplement of the campaign.

León Romero's contribution came with a printed piece; a hand-stitched publication to communicate the campaign in the different retail outlets through an offline medium.

The publication showcases three photographic reports with the main characters of the campaign; Christian Meier, a former professional World Tour Rider, David Gonzalez, custom bike designer and the Colombo brothers, owners and chefs of different iconic restaurants in Barcelona.

There is a strong typographic presence in the editorial piece, with distinct references to 'road type signage', emphasising the link between the main characters and the pavement. This typographic approach is combined with an edgy page layout, with pictures and texts arranged in a dynamic and loose way to display their day-to-day life.

The publication also has a small insert to point out some of the attributes of Levi's new technology, in parallel with a singer sewn finish to refer to the classic stitch of their legendary jeans.

Stretch

# Pirate

Only / onlystudio.co.uk
🌐 UK

With around the clock access to over 600 studios worldwide and professional standard spaces at an affordable price, Pirate are changing the game; making creative space accessible to all. Branding agency Only's job was to capture the spirit at the heart of the brand and create an identity that puts the artist community first.

"Focus on the things that matter. Get the basics right. That's the Pirate way."

*Arial* was selected as the brand's corporate typeface – freely licensed and accessible to all. Only stripped away the corporate logo to emphasise the URL. They hijacked the sound recording symbol ℗ to act as a digital shorthand, using a glyph from the *Arial* typeface. Clear and direct. Against the status quo.

Applications use three settings of typographic stretch to create a distinctive aesthetic. At locations around the world, place names are free-stretched on exterior frontages. Interior wayfinding repurposes an off-the-shelf modular racking system, reducing fit-out costs through an ownable and consistent approach.

**Photography:** Marcus Ginns (London) / Andy Wang (Los Angeles).

# LETTERING

*Contributing Designers:* The Office of Ordinary Things • Campbell Hay • Swear Words INTERVIEW • Wedge • BOND • Atelier Baudelaire • GeneralPublic Studio • Bielke&Yang • Pràctica →

Lettering

# Byte Bars

**The Office of Ordinary Things / ot.studio**
🌐 USA

Competing in a saturated snack bar market, The Office of Ordinary Things developed a strategy for Byte Bars that subverts stereotypical "crunchy granola" aesthetics. The outcome is a brand that appeals to a younger generation with a bold identity and light-hearted irreverence. Representing a cross-generational, free-spirited vibe, the shapes of the type and icons are influenced by the groovy 1960s and the vivid colour palette is drawn from the electric poppiness of the 80s and early 90s.

Lettering

# The Art Studio

Campbell Hay / campbellhay.com
🌐 UK

The Art Studio is a purpose-built block within a London junior school. The new building will provide an inspiring space for children to express themselves creatively.

Campbell Hay has created a playful and bold brand identity using a set of geometric shapes as building blocks. The identity includes artworks created by the children.

Applied across various brand communications, the shapes have been used to form letters, words, drawings and patterns, as well as a tiled installation that will become an integral part of the building's surface.

# Birra Zonzo

Swear Words / swearwords.com.au
Australia

Zonzo means 'to wander' in Italian and their ambling, shifting wordmark forms the core idea of this super-flexible brand. An offshoot of their wine business, Birra Zonzo represents the playful, energetic nephew of the family. Colourful, floating letterforms, self-merchandising cartons and naive little illustrations bring the party to this delicious beer.

# INTERVIEW
## Swear Words / Scott Larritt

swearwords.com.au
🌐 Australia

Gym Snack Bar

Swear Words is an Australian creative studio specialising in brand identity and packaging design. They are committed to producing environmentally conscious solutions that are as engaging as they are functional. They believe that great design behaves like a swear word — a succinct and passionate communication of your story.

### What is your background and how did you become involved in graphic design?

There's nothing unique about my career path from liberal arts major to ski bum/hospitality worker to graphic designer. However, I had a pretty interesting upbringing moving around between New Zealand, the USA and Australia. Growing up I was obsessed with 90's street art and NFL and college football team liveries. On reflection, these were my introductions to bold type and colour, two things that tend to pervade my studio's work today.

I started Swear Words with my original business partner straight out of university in 2003. Due to our personal passions for drinking and eating, we found an immediate niche in the food and beverage sector and still work with some of these first clients today.

### How would you describe your creative style and process?

I like to think that we don't really have a style. Our solutions are driven by each project's requirements. That said, we hear from clients that there is an overriding DNA in our work that has an approachable quality, a sense of quiet confidence born of simplicity and warmth — I'm happy with that description.

Mostly working with small to medium-sized businesses, we can talk directly with the owners or founders whose passion tends to shine through — being able to discover this and communicate it well creates a great visual identity.

### Typography has a strong prominence in your portfolio. Why is type so important to your work?

You really can say it all with type. For me, an identity usually starts with a logotype and supporting typestyles and sometimes that's all you need. The functionality and simplicity of type-based solutions really stand out on shelves and screens. For our clients, who are generally competing directly with other brands, this is really important.

### How would you define good typography?

I think good typography is thoughtful — whether it's appropriate or wildly inappropriate, both examples are compelling. I like type that's unexpected just as much as type that's perfectly harmonious and functional. For me, type becomes good when it has a reason for being and it supports a broader narrative through considered execution of font style, scale and colour.

### Do you have a favourite font and why?

Being a New Zealander I'm biased but I think pretty much anything that Kris Sowersby does at Klim Type Foundry is great. I'm particularly fond of *Founders Grotesk Text*. The mixture of refinement and approachability in this typeface makes it suitable for so many applications. It has a personality, doesn't take itself too seriously, but can also put on a suit and tie if needed.

↑ Kura Kura
 Pod & Parcel
 Doghouse

Lettering

206

**How often is typography used as the starting point for your design work?**
Depending on the job, the majority of our designs start with type. With packaging design for retail, messaging hierarchy is super-important. We often figure out the logotype and overall type system first, then move onto colour, imagery and other supporting graphic devices to help define ranges and further improve the information hierarchy.

**How can effective design enhance a brand's identity?**
Effective design creates a unique voice. A brand with a unique voice is more likely to get noticed, you're more likely to stop and listen to what it has to say. This makes all the difference.

**What are your main goals and considerations when working on the design of beverage identities and their labelling?**
Ultimately our goal is to design a package that you can't help but pick up. We consider the shape, colour and flexibility of the brand elements to be the highest priorities. You may not be able to read a brand from 10 metres away, but you should be able to easily distinguish its shape and colour. I guess this is why we are drawn towards bold, colourful typographic solutions.

**What do you think of the design scene in Australia today? How has it evolved?**
I feel like there are a lot of great design studios in Australia but from my perspective, the scene is now more of a global one.

A lot of our clients are international or have global aspirations. It's easier than ever to seek us out and because of that I believe we, as are many other Australian design studios, are now on a level playing field with the rest of the world.

← TOJI Sake

# Gym Snack Bar

Big Type

Swear Words / swearwords.com.au
⊕ Australia

Not everyone wants to go to the gym, but a lot of us want to snack better without resorting to celery!

 With the design for Gym, Swear Words combined familiar colours and an unexpectedly playful, voluptuous wordmark to communicate wellness without subscribing to health and fitness snack bar stereotypes.

 Using scale and repetition, the Gym package jumps off the shelf to create a focal point in the category.

# Swirl

**Wedge / wedge.work**
🌐 Canada

Swirl is a plant-based ice cream brand from Montreal, Canada. They sought a youthful, bold expression that doesn't say 'vegan' when you think 'vegan'. Its founders are inspired by bold streetwear symbols, and wanted an original logo and pack that could stand out and be iconic. The curvaceous custom mark is inspired by the wickedly smooth texture of Swirl's ice cream. Drawn by hand then digitally perfected, the artwork sparked a total rebrand.

Lettering

# Xnet

BOND / bond-agency.com
🌐 Estonia

Brand refresh and development for Xnet, a Latvian e-store with renewed, bold ambitions. Now equally boldly standing for emotion and self-expression. Because: "Even in these confusing times, life — and shopping — is not only about survival or fulfilling one's simplest needs. It's about values and wants. It's about *the X you want. Tas X, ko tu meklē.*" Just look deep into the spiral and you'll feel it.

The identity is headlined by an audacious wordmark built from custom-crafted letter shapes, also allowing the letter 'X' to be used as a standalone symbol and as a background element when needed.

Big Type

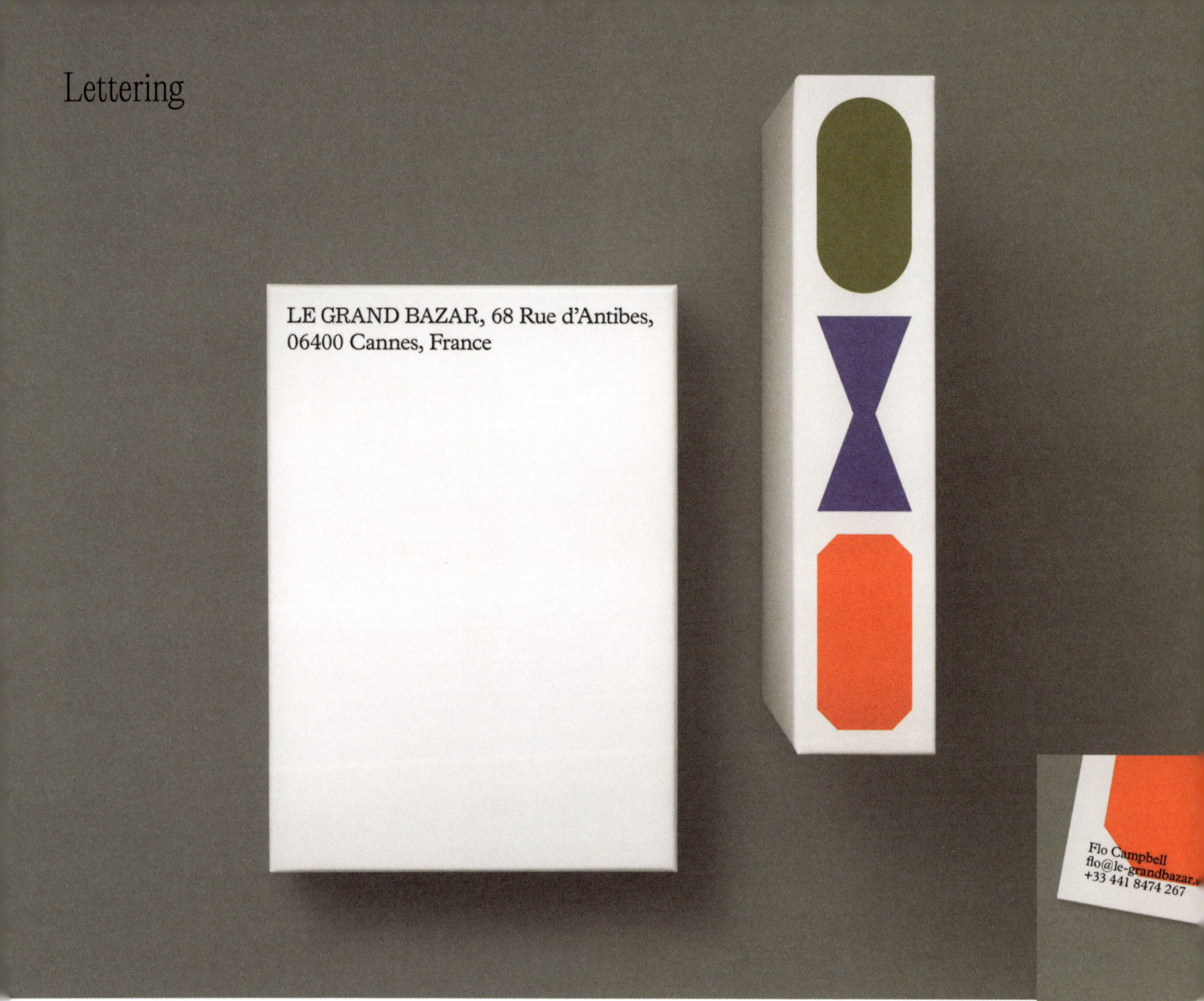

Lettering

# Le Grand Bazar

**Campbell Hay / campbellhay.com**
⊕ UK

Ever since it first opened more than 20 years ago, Le Grand Bazar has been the South of France's destination for carefully curated designer fashion. Under the direction of a new generation, the boutique approached Campbell Hay to create a new, contemporary brand proposition which paid homage to its heritage while engaging a new generation with an avant-garde, future-facing vision.

    The resulting identity system was rooted in the boutique's iconic location. The logo was composed around the address, well known far beyond the city's limits. Dusky, riviera-coloured geometric forms, loosely inspired by the dressmaker's patterns, established a playful, dynamic component.

Big Type

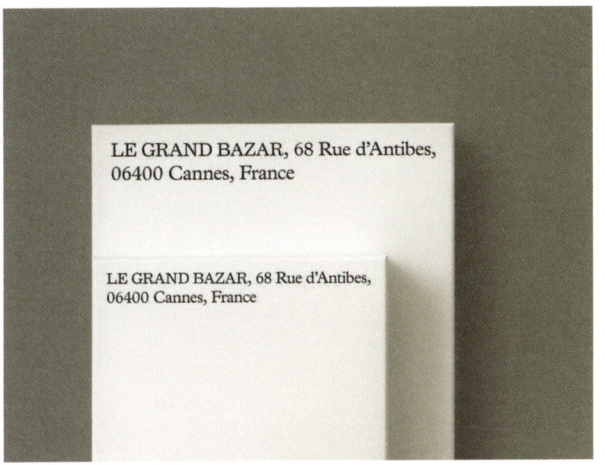

Lettering

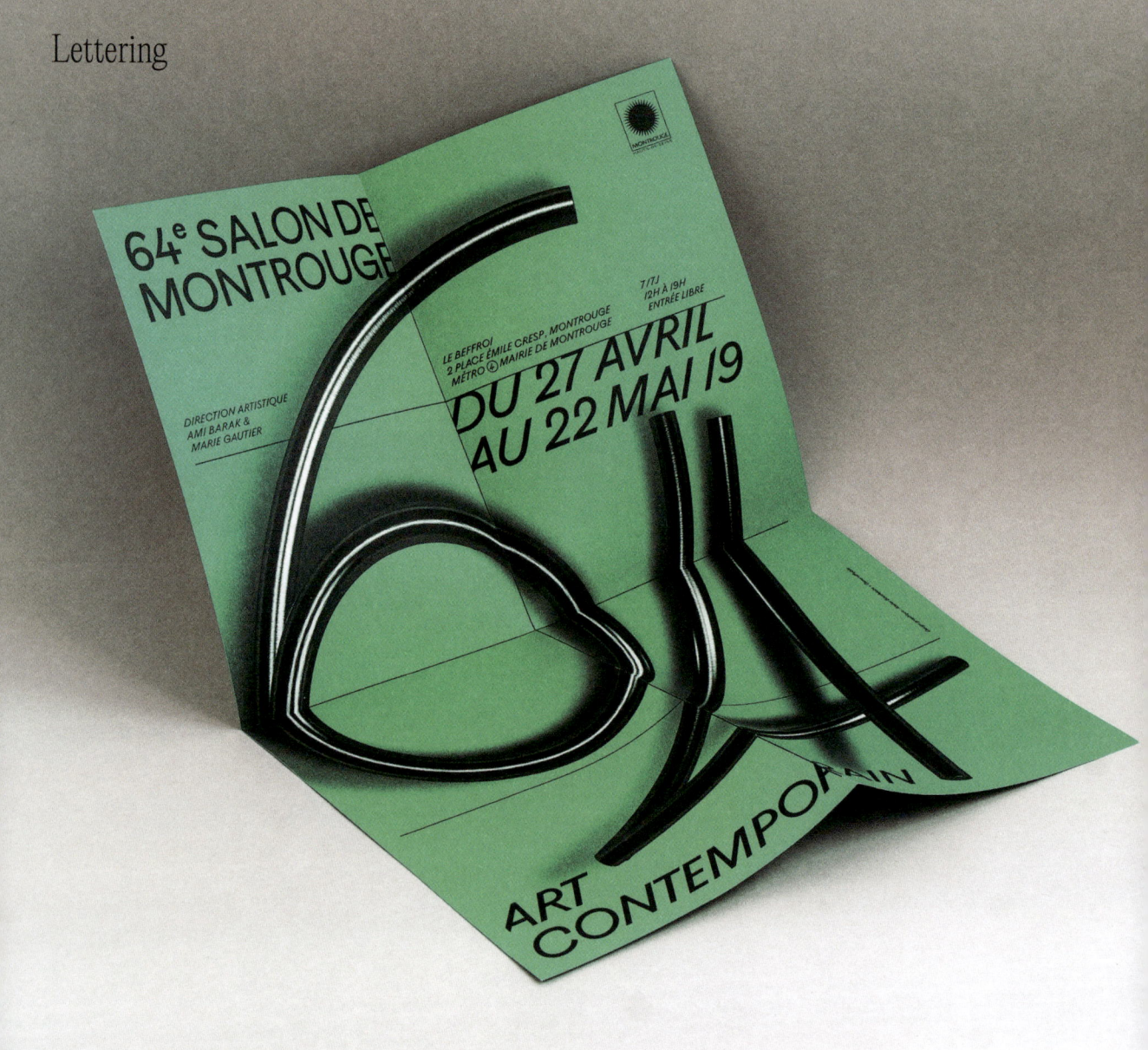

# 64ᵉ Salon de Montrouge

**Atelier Baudelaire x GeneralPublic Studio / atelierbaudelaire.com generalpublic.fr**
⊕ **France**

*Salon de Montrouge* is an annual contemporary art exhibition, dedicated to international emerging artists. Each year the identity is based on a bold colour and a specific 3D-like type design for the iconic number of the art fair. For the fourth year in a row, the identity features the number of this edition in volume, in an even more sculptural spirit. Composed of simple modules placed on a grid, this monumental number unfolds its geometric shapes on the different supporting communications. Atelier Baudelaire x GeneralPublic Studio have been developing a technique to print 3D visuals with different Pantone colours, to achieve a strong impact of colour through a powerful palette of intense green, black and silver.

Big Type

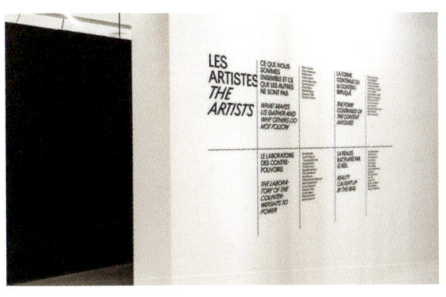
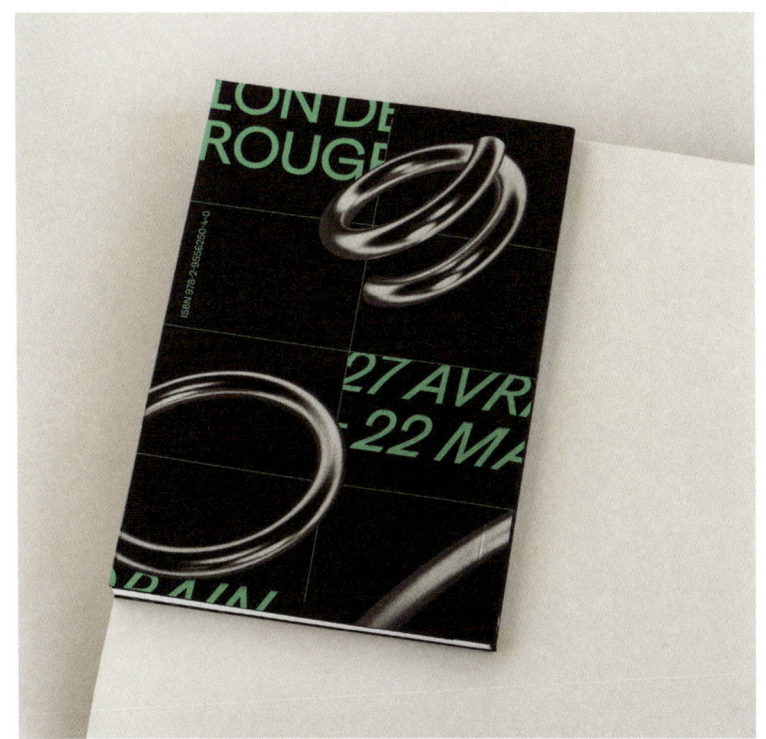

# Lettering

Big Type

## Talormade

**Bielke&Yang / bielkeyang.com**
🌐 Norway

Bielke&Yang wanted to create an identity that reflected Talor Browne's unique personality and project. Since Talor has paved the way for women in a segment dominated by men, they looked to historic women's rights material for inspiration. Talor refuses to be told what she can do and not do. Bielke&Yang wanted Talormade's new identity to reflect this, to stand out, just as much as she does herself. They have brought this personality through at every opportunity. It's all about creating safe inclusive spaces where people can enjoy delicious doughnuts and coffee but most of all, have fun!

**Photography:** Lars Petter Pettersen / Tommy Andresen.

# Lettering

Big Type

# ZETAK

Pràctica / practica.design
🌐 Spain

This visual identity was created for ZETAK, a Basque electronic music project by Pello Reparaz. The project explores new boundaries reinterpreting Euskal Herria's traditional music to generate new sounds.

Coming from ZETAK's nature Pràctica designed *Arbizu*, a custom typeface conceived under the same idea. Based on documentation research, ancient characters from the Basque alphabet have been rescued and juxtaposed with a sans serif typeface of today, resulting in a contemporary view of the traditional Basque imagery.

Each *Arbizu* character contains three alternates that are set randomly, giving musicality and rhythm to the typeface.

**Typeface Production:** Jordi Embodas.
**Photography:** Kiwi Bravo.

223

© 2025 Counter-Print
counter-print.co.uk
info@counter-print.co.uk

**British Library cataloguing-in-publication data:** A catalogue of this book can be found in the British Library.

**ISBN:** 978-1-8381865-7-9

First published in the United Kingdom in 2022. Reprinted in 2023 and 2025.

Edited and produced by Counter-Print.

**Design:** Jon Dowling & Céline Leterme

**Typefaces:** Quench and Editorial New

**Printing and Binding:** 1010 Printing International Limited, China

Copyright on projects and their related imagery is held by the respective design agencies.

All rights reserved. No part of this book may be reproduced, stored in a retrieval system, or transmitted in any form or by any means without prior written permission from the publisher.